How to use

In this issue

The 90 daily readings in this issue of *Explore* are designed to help you understand and apply the Bible as you read it each day.

It's serious!

We suggest that you allow 15 minutes each day to work through the Bible passage with the notes. It should be a meal, not a snack! Readings from other parts of the Bible can throw valuable light on the study passage. These cross-references can be skipped if you are already feeling full up, but they will expand your grasp of the Bible. *Explore* uses the NIV Bible translation, but you can also use it with the ESV or another translation of your choice.

Sometimes a prayer section will encourage you to stop and pray through the application of God's word—but it is always important to allow time to pray for God's Spirit to bring his word to life, and to shape the way we think and live.

We're serious!

All of us who work on *Explore* share a passion for getting the Bible into people's lives. We passionately hold to the Bible as God's word—to honour and follow, not to explain away.

1 Find a time you can read the Bible each day

2 Find a place where you can be quiet and think

3 Ask God to help you understand

4 Carefully read through the Bible passage for today

5 Study the verses with Explore, taking time to think

6 Pray about what you have read

thegoodbook
COMPANY

Opening up the Bible

Welcome to Explore

Being a Christian isn't a skill you learn, like carpentry or flower arranging. Nor is it a lifestyle choice, like the kind of clothes you wear, or the people you choose to hang out with. It's about having a real relationship with the living God through his Son, Jesus Christ. The Bible tells us that this relationship is like a marriage.

It's important to start with this, because many Christians view the practice of daily Bible-reading as a Christian duty, or a hard discipline that is just one more thing to get done in our busy modern lives.

But the Bible is God speaking to us: opening his mind to us on how he thinks, what he wants for us and what his plans are for the world. And most importantly, it tells us what he has done for us in sending his Son, Jesus Christ, into the world. It's the way the Spirit shows Jesus to us, and changes us as we behold his glory.

The Bible is not a manual. It's a love letter. And as with any love letter, we'll want to treasure it, and make time to read and re-read it, so we know we are loved, and discover how we can please the one who loves us. Here are a few suggestions for making your daily time with God more of a joy than a burden:

💙 *Time:* Find a time when you will not be disturbed, and when the cobwebs are cleared from your mind. Many people have found that the morning is the best time as it sets you up for the day. If you're not a "morning person", then last thing at night or a mid-morning break might suit you. Whatever works for you is right for you.

💙 *Place:* Jesus says that we are not to make a great show of our religion *(see Matthew 6:5-6)*, but rather, to pray with the door to our room shut. Some people plan to get to work a few minutes earlier and get their Bible out in an office or some other quiet corner.

💙 *Prayer:* Although *Explore* helps with specific prayer ideas from the passage, try to develop your own lists to pray through. Use the flap inside the back cover to help with this. And allow what you read in the Scriptures to shape what you pray for yourself, the world and others.

💙 *Share:* As the saying goes—*expression deepens impression.* So try to cultivate the habit of sharing with others what you have learned. Why not join our Facebook group to share your encouragements, questions and prayer requests? Search for *Explore: For your daily walk with God.*

And remember, *it's quality, not quantity, that counts:* better to think briefly about a single verse than to skim through pages without absorbing anything. It's about developing your relationship with the living God. The sign that your daily time with God is real is when you start to love him more and serve him more wholeheartedly.

Tim Thornborough and Carl Laferton
Editors

Fear in the new year

Was your new year happy, or utterly stressful? If the latter, how can you bring this honestly to God in prayer? And how can we talk to the Lord about the year ahead?

Anguish

Read Psalm 55:1-8

❓ *What is the psalmist asking God to do (v 1)?* To listen to his prayer

❓ *How does he describe his feelings (v 2, 4-5)?* His thoughts are troubled, feels + distraught

❓ *Note the different images. What does this suggest to you about his state?*

❓ *What has caused these feelings (v 3)?*

❓ *What does he long to do (v 6-8)?*
Fly away from all his anguish + be at rest.

Lament

Lament psalms arise out of difficult situations. In them, the psalmist honestly expresses his feelings and problems to God, sometimes in extreme ways. In this psalm we see someone who is on the edge; their mind in overdrive, restless and confused, hypersensitive—what one writer describes as an extreme anxiety attack. The amazing thing that laments like this show us is that we can bring all of our thoughts, feelings and worries to God—*all of them!* It's ok to tell God that I'm not ok.

TIME OUT

Read Psalm 139, especially v 1, 4, 22-23. Amazingly, knowing all this about us, he still loves us, and *will* still love us if we tell him exactly how we feel. God loves the truth.

Betrayal

Read Psalm 55:9-14

The reason for David's anguish is that someone is verbally attacking him (v 3, 9, 12).

❓ *Who is this attacker, and why would this be particularly painful (v 12-14)?*
Close friend + companion is attacking him

Even Jesus was betrayed by a close friend (see Matthew 26:47-50). He knows how this feels. The words of this psalm may have particular resonance with anyone who has been abused or betrayed by a partner, friend or family member. It could be a way to express their anguish and to reach out to God.

☑ Apply

❓ *Have you ever felt like this? If not, do you know someone who has?*

❓ *How might this psalm encourage you in such a situation?* God loves us & listens to us – He will always be there for us in every situation.

▲ Pray

Honestly express to God how you are feeling right now. Don't hold back. Feel the freedom to pour it out before your Father who knows and loves you.

And pray on behalf of others. As I write this, Ukrainian cities are being destroyed, and African churches burned out. Stand alongside them in anguish before the Lord, who listens and loves.

An unburdened future

As well as pouring out our feelings about difficult situations to the Lord, we can also plead with God to act. This is what the psalmist does in the rest of this psalm.

Read Psalm 55:15-23

Lament flows from faith: the conviction that God is relevant to every situation. He loves us, and he can make a difference. This is why we plead with him to act. Lament is not the sign of a weak believer. David, Jeremiah, Job and other heroes of faith lamented.

He asks for *what*?

❓ *What does the psalmist ask for (v 15)?*

❓ *Would you be comfortable asking God to do this?*

❓ *Where and how do you see the psalmist expressing trust in God in these verses?*

This request may shock us. We need to remember that this imprecation (a spoken curse) is part of a lament spoken by someone in the depths of anguish, honestly expressing a desire for vengeance. By expressing this desire, the psalmist is choosing to hand his vengeance over to God, rather than taking revenge himself— for example by answering verbal attack with verbal attack. Note that in verses 19-23 it is *God* who is asked to act. Strangely enough, this is part of trusting in God, the God who is totally just, and powerful, and ultimately will see justice done.

···· **TIME OUT** ·····································

Read Romans 12:14-21

❓ *Where is the "handing over" of vengeance in this passage?*

❓ *What can this lead to (v 14, 20-21)?*

···

This imprecation is not an excuse for us to be negative about others when we are feeling fine. However, in horribly difficult times it is a way to hand over our existing feelings to God, helping us to live in God's love.

Casting burdens
Read Psalm 55:22 again

❓ *What commands and promises are there in this precious verse?*

❓ *What is involved in "casting burdens" do you think?*

▲ Pray

Do you have any deep-seated desires for revenge that you need to hand over to God? Then do it now.

What burden are you carrying into 2023 that you can now cast on him?

Give yourself enough time to do this. Neither of these things are easy.

And pray for those you know who are wrestling with the pain of injustice, or bearing crushing burdens, that they would be able to know the reality of God's care for them and trust him with their deepest hurts.

Who will you fear?

This is a psalm that holds fear and trust in tension. The psalmist fears humans, but trusts in God. How does this apply to you as 2023 starts?

....

Fear and trust

Read Psalm 56:1-13

> ❷ *What exactly is the psalmist afraid of?*
> ❷ *What exactly is the psalmist trusting in?*

The repeated refrain in verses 3-4 and 10-11 contains some key truths. Trust is not just for when things are going well (that's easy), but also for when things are difficult. We can still trust when we are afraid because we trust in the ultimately trustworthy God. But this trust isn't a passive thing—it requires us to call out to God for help (v 1, 7-9.)

Word and promise

Many people view prayer as an act of weakness or desperation—whispering or shrieking our hopes to the silent heavens.

> ❷ *How is Christian prayer different (v 4)?*

The psalm gives us one clue — see "whose word I praise". We can trust God because he gives us his word, and he has demonstrated time and time again how he keeps his word and his promises.

···· **TIME OUT** ·······································

God gives many immediate promises in the Bible. However, he also gives long-term promises which form the basis of his relationship with his people.

He promised Abraham descendants, land,

a relationship, and blessing for all nations (Genesis 12:1-3). He promised David that one of his descendants would always rule (2 Samuel 7:8-15). Both promises were ultimately fulfilled in Jesus (Galatians 3:8, 14; Acts 13:32-34). If you want to learn more, look for books that explain the big story of the Bible. One example would be Vaughan Roberts' *God's Big Picture*.

What can mere mortals do to me?

Read Psalm 56:10-13

> ❷ *What assurance does he come to?*
> ❷ *What commitment does he make (v 13)?*

In one sense, mortals can do quite a lot to us, and the psalmist knows it first-hand (v 1-2, 5-6, 8)! How, then, can he say, "What can mere mortals do to me" (v 4, 11)? The truth here is that humans can do nothing about what ultimately matters—our relationship and destiny with God.

⌃ Pray

Thank God for his promises to all believers, and the security that we have in him, even when we are struggling with painful things.

Resolve before the Lord to walk before God in the light of life this year.

JUDGES: Light in the dark

Life for believers in a broken world can often feel very dark—but even in those times God is at work.

Getting our bearings

The book of Judges is a treasure trove of gripping stories. Many of its characters are well known—people like Gideon, Samson, Deborah; others like Shamgar, Othniel and Tola are not. Judges describes glorious rescues, dramatic exploits, but also terrible events. Some of the darkest episodes in the Bible are found in this book.

Read Joshua 24:14-15, 21 and Judges 21:25

- ❓ *What do the people commit to at the end of the book of Joshua?*
- ❓ *What are the people like by the end of Judges?*

The book of Judges tells the story of God's people after the death of Joshua, when they have started to settle in the promised land, and before the arrival of Samuel, roughly 300 years of history. Sadly, the book describes a downward spiral into deeper sin by God's people as they forsake their God. But through it all, God is faithful to his people, even in their sin. Light shines even in the darkest times.

A promising start
Read Judges 1:1-8

- ❓ *What do the Israelites plan to do?*
- ❓ *What is good about how they do it?*
- ❓ *What does the writer say is the real reason for their victories (v 4)?*

✓ Apply

The death of Joshua left a huge hole in the leadership of God's people.

- ❓ *But what do these opening verses teach us about where true leadership and security is to be found for God's people?*
- ❓ *How might this help us when godly leaders die or move on; or when leaders let us down and fail?*

God is faithful to his promises in Judges 1.

- ❓ *Where can you see God's faithfulness to his promises in your life, even in dark times?*
- ❓ *How might that encourage you today?*

More success! But...
Read Judges 1:9-21

- ❓ *What successes do God's people achieve in these verses?*
- ❓ *Again, what is the key to their success (v 19)?*
- ❓ *What warning notes are sounded in verses 19 and 21?*

▲ Pray

Pray that through these studies in Judges, God would encourage you and teach you about his faithfulness and commitment to his people.

Where it all went wrong

What happens when we compromise on obedience to God's commands? Judges 1 shows us the sad consequences…

Judges begins with life after Joshua. And it started well. Enemies defeated, land taken, the people united and dependant on God for victory. But it's not long before things begin to go wrong.

Danger of compromise

Read Judges 1:22-36

- ❓ *What is the consistent pattern in these verses as the different tribes try to take the land?*
- ❓ *What different ways does the writer use to describe the relationships between the Israelites and the various peoples of Canaan?*
- ❓ *How would you sum up the situation in the land at the end of chapter 1?*

Look up Deuteronomy 7:1-6

- ❓ *What were the people to do to the nations in the land?*
- ❓ *What reasons did God give for this?*

These commands might feel wrong to us today. But God's people in the Old Testament were a specific nation in a specific place. God used his people to bring his judgment on the inhabitants of the land. Previously he'd been merciful and allowed these nations to thrive; and some individuals had even trusted in God! But now his just judgment was to be meted out through his people. This is very different for God's people today—we're a people scattered throughout all the nations of the world. Our job is not to bring judgment through the sword; we are instead to bring the gospel of Jesus so that the nations will be spared the ultimate judgment of God!

✓ Apply

In not doing what God commanded, Israel compromised, and the polluting nations remained among them, causing God's people to be led astray. The rest of the Old Testament, including Judges, tells the story.

- ❓ *How might you be tempted to compromise when faced with difficult commands?*
- ❓ *How do the views of the world around you affect your thinking and actions?*

God's verdict

Read Judges 2:1-5

- ❓ *What had God promised the people? What did he want them to do?*
- ❓ *What is God's response to their disobedience?*
- ❓ *How do the people respond? Why aren't tears enough? See 2:11-13!*

⌃ Pray

Ask God to help you to be faithful to him, and repent of your sinful compromises honestly and wholeheartedly.

The pattern is set

The choices one generation makes have consequences for the next. Is there any escape from the cycle?

We saw in chapter 1 that the people of God started well in seeking to settle in the land. They drove out some of their enemies whilst seeking God's guidance. But chapter 1 also showed how the people compromised with the nations. They failed to drive out many of the people, and ended up living side by side with them. Chapter 2 shows the consequences with an overview of the years ahead. Chapter 2 sets the pattern which the rest of the book follows.

Sin has consequences

Read Judges 2:6-16

- ❓ *How did the people behave in the lifetime of Joshua (v 6-9)?*
- ❓ *How do the next generation behave (v 10-13)?*
- ❓ *What is at the heart of this behaviour according to the writer in verse 10?*
- ❓ *How does the writer highlight how serious this is in verses 12-13?*
- ❓ *What is God's reaction (v 14-15)?*

☑ Apply

These verses highlight how quickly God's people can forsake him through compromising with the world around and forgetting him.

- ❓ *Why is forgetfulness so dangerous for Christians?*
- ❓ *What Bible truths are you in most danger of forgetting at the moment?*

❓ *What do you think it means to "know the Lord" in verse 10? How is knowing God and growth in him vital for spiritual health and protection?*

One issue for Israel seems to have been that they were not teaching the next generation about the Lord.

- ❓ *Why is it vital we teach our children and young people at home and in church about the Lord (for help look up Deuteronomy 6:20-25)?*
- ❓ *Judges 2:16 is a ray of hope. What does this verse teach about the Lord, despite human sin?*

Down, down, down…

Read Judges 2:17 – 3:6

- ❓ *How do these verses set the pattern for God's people for the years to come?*
- ❓ *How does God use the presence of the nations in the land (2:22 and 3:1, 4)?*
- ❓ *Do you think Israel passed or failed the test (3:5-6)?*

Remember Deuteronomy 7:3-4 for how serious this is!

⌃ Pray

Pray for God's grace to know him better and to fight sin. Pray for children and young people in your family and church to come to know the Lord and stand for him.

❤ *Bible in a year: Genesis 16-17 • Romans 6*

God is the hero!

Think of the most exceptional leader you know of. What are their qualities? What are their limitations?

....

Who's in charge?

Leadership is a big issue in the book of Judges. The book begins with the death of a gifted leader, Joshua (1:1), and ends with the comment that people did what they wanted because they had no obvious leader (21:25).

Judges weren't law-court officials as we know them—they were people raised up by God to lead God's people and rescue them from their enemies. But behind each of them was God himself. We're not meant to see the judges as examples for us. Some of them lived very messy lives and made very bad decisions! Rather, they teach us about God—the real Saviour. The book of Judges shows us our sin and points to our need for a Saviour.

A model judge

Read Judges 3:7-11

- ❷ *Looking at the passage as a whole, what pattern can you see in the story that we first noted in chapter 2?*
- ❷ *In Judges 3:7-8, what did the Israelites do and how did God respond?*
- ❷ *What are the next stages of the cycle in verses 9-10?*
- ❷ *What do we learn about Othniel here? Why might it be significant that he is the first judge?*
- ❷ *Remember Judges 1:9-13. How had Othniel resisted the temptations of 3:6?*

❷ *What is the result of the rescue (v 11)?*

The model Saviour

We might at first think Judges 3:7-11 is all about Othniel, but in fact Othniel is simply the Lord's instrument to save his people.

Read Judges 3:7-11 again

- ❷ *What do you learn about God's reaction to sin?*
- ❷ *How do you see his mercy and grace at work?*

Notice in verse 10 the first mention of the Spirit of God in Judges. We'll see later that God often gives the judges his Spirit to empower them to save his people from their enemies.

☑ Apply

We learn little about Othniel, but much about God. And Othniel points us to Jesus, our perfect Saviour.

- ❷ *As you consider your own life, what do these verses teach you about the danger of sin in verse 7?*
- ❷ *And what do they teach you about how God delights to rescue sinners like us?*

Praise God for his mercy in Jesus!

Faithful refuge

When disaster strikes, where do we find refuge? For the psalmist, it is God—the ultimate source of rest and security.

Read Psalm 57:1-11

- ❷ *Where does the psalmist take refuge and why (v 1)?*
- ❷ *How does he describe God (v 2-3, 10)?*
- ❷ *How does he describe his enemies and their acts (v 3, 4, 6)?*
- ❷ *Beyond his please in verse 1, how will he respond to all of this—(v 7-9)?*

The psalmist has to live among people who act like wild beasts, whose words are as dangerous and hurtful as weapons of war (v 4). Yet, he has a refuge in God—the God who will vindicate him (v 2) and turn the violence of his enemies back upon them (v 6).

Sticks and Stones?

Look back at the attacks in Psalm 55:3, 9, 12, and in Psalm 56:5. Many of them are verbal (as here). The Bible doesn't agree that "words will never hurt me". Instead, it recognises the anguish that they can cause. Therefore, it also warns us to be careful how we speak.

···· **TIME OUT** ·······································

Read James 3:1-12

- ❷ *How does this passage describe the tongue?*
- ❷ *How does this challenge Christians about the way we speak?*

⌃ Pray

Ask God to help you and all Christians to speak truthfully and with kindness.

Loving, steadfast, faithful

Why can the psalmist be confident that God will be his refuge? Because of God's character. This psalm uses two words to describe this: "love" and "faithfulness" (v 3, 10). The first includes the ideas of love, steadfastness, loyalty. The second includes the ideas of truth and faithfulness.

This is why the psalmist can be steadfast even under attack (v 7). This is why he will praise his God even at night (v 8) and among the nations (v 9). We remember Paul and Silas singing to God in the Philippian jail, (perhaps this very psalm?) because they knew what the psalmist knew. They knew that the God who is above all creation (v 5, 11) acts within creation (v 3). And we remember how God acted on that occasion—truly their refuge (see Acts 16:22-26)!

⌃ Pray

Thank God that he is our refuge, that he is full of steadfast love and true faithfulness. If you need it, seek him as your refuge now. If you don't, pray for those who do.

An unlikely saviour

Sometimes, Bible rescues are achieved through the most surprising of people.

A tragicomic tale

In Judges 3 we meet Eglon and Ehud. Lots of the stories in Judges are dark and sad, but the way this narrative is told is surely meant to make us smile. But at first, the story is deadly serious.

Read Judges 3:12-31

❷ *What familiar cycle is described in verses 12-15?*

❷ *Why is it significant to read in verse 12 that God "gave" Eglon power over Israel (remember 3:8)?*

❷ *What does this cycle remind us about the state of the human heart and the need for God's grace and mercy?*

❷ *What does it teach us about God's view of sin and its consequences?*

Ehud is an unlikely saviour. Verse 15 describes him as left-handed. Soldiers traditionally fought right-handed, and this was their strength. To be left-handed was thought to be a disadvantage, even weak. Ehud was also from the tribe of Benjamin, one of the weakest tribes and already a military failure (1:21). But he is God's choice, and that is what makes the difference.

❷ *What elements of the story in verses 16-26 are surprising and unexpected?*

❷ *What overall picture do we get of Eglon?*

❷ *How does this highlight the tragedy of Eglon ruling over Israel for 18 years?*

❷ *How does the end of the story in verses 27-30 highlight God's judgment and power over his enemies, and God's grace to his people?*

A surprising saviour!

Ehud (and indeed Shamgar in verse 31) is a surprising saviour. But like all the judges, we're not meant to copy him. He's flawed and weak. These judges keep pointing us forward to a better Saviour—Jesus! But Jesus, too, is an unlikely Saviour.

Read 1 Corinthians 1:18-25

❷ *Why is the message about Jesus such foolishness to ears of the world?*

❷ *Why is the cross the power of God, according to Paul (v 21)?*

☑ Apply

❷ *How does the unlikely way God saves through Ehud and through Jesus highlight God's power?*

❷ *What does the cross do to our pride and the thought that we're the powerful masters of our lives?*

❷ *Why is it that we are sometimes ashamed of the message of the cross, even though it's God's way of salvation and wisdom?*

Thank God for the wisdom and power of the cross.

An unwilling leader

Why is it that God's people often find it hard to do what he says? Is it fear? Is it the cost? Or perhaps it's just a sense of resignation that we can't change the situation…

Same old, same old

God's people need a hero again. But this time Judges 4 presents a rather reluctant hero. God's people are in the same situation again after the death of Ehud. Once again, we're presented with a familiar cycle we've seen before.

Read Judges 4:1-16

- ❷ What familiar features do we see in verses 1-3?
- ❷ In what ways is this time different from 3:8 and 3:14?
- ❷ What is Deborah's role in 4:4-7?
- ❷ How is Barak portrayed in verses 8-10?
- ❷ Despite Barak's misgivings, what is the outcome of the battle in verses 11-16 and who is really responsible?

✔ Apply

Barak is an ambiguous figure. He looks weak in some ways, but…

Read 1 Samuel 12:11 and Hebrews 11:32-33

- ❷ What encouragement might this give us about the way God uses weak and fearful people like us?
- ❷ In what specific areas might you be unwilling to obey God's word in your life?
- ❷ What are the reasons why you find it hard to obey him?

God defeats his enemies

Read Judges 4:17-24

Sisera flees the battle on foot (v 17).

- ❷ How does he meet his end? Why is it significant that Jael is the one who delivers the fatal blow (v 9)?
- ❷ Why is it significant that Barak is mentioned in verse 22?

✔ Apply

It's easy to read a passage like this, and feel that we too let God down and fail him through fear, lack of courage, weak hearts and a whole host of other reasons. But the writer reminds us that God is the real hero (see v 6, 9, 14, 15 and 23). And wonderfully we have a better Saviour who knows how we feel, but didn't sin.

Read Hebrews 4:14-16

- ❷ What encouragement does the writer give us in these verses? What does he urge us to do?

⌃ Pray

Spend some time confessing your own weaknesses to the Lord, and admitting the times you've let him down. Ask for his forgiveness, and rejoice in his love and acceptance of you in Jesus. Ask him for help to live his way today.

Whose side are you on?

What are your favourite songs to sing? What are those songs all about?

Judges 5 is a unique chapter in this book. It's a song of victory penned by Deborah and Barak all about how God defeated the enemies of God's people during the events of Judges 4. But it's also a song that highlights those who didn't come to help the people of God in trouble. Those who came to fight on God's behalf are his friends. Those who didn't are classed as enemies. God's friends are shown to be those who line up behind his cause and who are prepared to fight for his glory.

Sing God's praises

Read Judges 5:1-15

- ❓ *What's the main theme of the song (v 2)?*
- ❓ *What picture do verses 4-5 paint of God?*
- ❓ *What problem is sung about in verses 6-7 and how was it resolved?*
- ❓ *What do verses 10-15 describe God's faithful people doing?*

···· TIME OUT ·····························

"The One of Sinai" (v 5) is the God who revealed himself to Moses and God's people on Mount Sinai. To see what he's like, read **Exodus 19:16-18** and **34:1-7**.

- ❓ *Why is it significant that "the One of Sinai" is the same God who rescues his people in Judges 4 and 5?*

Enemies defeated

Read Judges 5:16-31

- ❓ *Verses 16-18 describe a different reaction to the events from some sections of God's people. What do they do?*
- ❓ *How does God see their decision (v 23)?*
- ❓ *What do you think about the brutal, gloating satire of verses 28-30?*

⌄ Apply

Judges 5 is fundamentally about God's glorious rescue of his people. He provides the leaders to save God's people. He is the one who leads his people to victory. But God's people have a choice—to line up behind their glorious saving Lord, or not!

- ❓ *When are you tempted to be ashamed of God and his plans, and not to "line up behind him"?*
- ❓ *What situations can you think of where you're tempted to put your own comfort before doing what is right for God and his kingdom?*

⌃ Pray

While we might be afraid and ashamed of God and his kingdom, we can know his forgiveness through Jesus. Spend some time confessing your fear and those times when his glory and priorities come second. Rejoice that there is forgiveness in Jesus.

Fleeces and fires

Gideon is a favourite Bible character for many. But is he an example we should follow, or a warning we should heed?

So far in Judges we've looked at Othniel, Ehud and Barak as the main characters of the story. Slowly but surely there has been a steady decline in their leadership. Othniel was a model judge, but Ehud and Barak had serious weaknesses. As we come to Gideon, we need to be cautious to use him as an example of faithfulness. He's God's man to save his people, but he's also terribly flawed. All the way through the book we need to remember that God is the Saviour, even if he uses flawed people for his saving purposes.

Yet more of the same!

Read Judges 6:1-10

- ❓ *Why did God's people suffer (v 1-6)?*
- ❓ *What is God's response to their cry (v 8)?*
- ❓ *How does God summarise the problem?*

The cycle we've seen before repeats itself, but this time there's a difference. The writer will spend a long time telling us about the preparation for Gideon's act of rescue.

A new hero?

Read Judges 6:11-32

The way God deals with Gideon is different to anyone else in Judges.

- ❓ *What unique experiences does Gideon have in verses 11, 12, 14, 16, 20, 21, 23, 25?*
- ❓ *What do you think should be the effect on Gideon of all these experiences?*

- ❓ *What do his responses show about him? See verses 13, 15, 17.*
- ❓ *How do the events of verses 25-32 show some progress in Gideon's heart?*

✔ Apply

Gideon is far from being the "mighty warrior" of verse 12!

- ❓ *But what does God's choice of Gideon show us about God and the way he works?*
- ❓ *How might that encourage you as you seek to serve God in your situation?*

For a New Testament perspective, have a look at 1 Corinthians 1:26-29.

Time for the fleece?

Read Judges 6:33-40

- ❓ *What do his requests to God about the fleece reveal about Gideon?*
- ❓ *Why are the fleeces unnecessary (v 14, 16, 36)?*
- ❓ *What do the fleece episodes reveal about God?*

⌃ Pray

Thank God for his patience and love for you, and his word to us in the Bible. Ask him to help you trust his sure word to guide you in all you face.

Outnumbered?

Gideon is ready for action. But who is it that really gives the victory? It is a wonderful story beloved by those who teach Bible stories to children!

But while the details are remarkable and memorable, we need to remember the big picture of Judges to see the desperate situation God's people were in because of their sin. The setting for this story is described in 6:1 and 6:6. Israel needs a saviour to rescue them from their enemies—and Gideon is the unlikely hero. Remember how the angel described him in 6:12. Is this really true? Has the story so far backed up the angel's word or not?

The 300

Read Judges 7:1-8

These verses describe the way God whittles down the army from 30,000 to 300.

> ❓ *Why did God do this (v 2, 7)?*
> ❓ *How do the armies of Israel and Midian compare now (see v 12)?*

···· **TIME OUT** ····································

Read Deuteronomy 20:1-9

> ❓ *How do these verses shed some light on what God asks of Gideon in Judges 7?*
> ❓ *What encouragement does God give in Deuteronomy 20:4?*

Whose victory?

Read Judges 7:9-25

The two armies are ridiculously uneven.

> ❓ *But what does God say to Gideon in verses 10-11? Why does God do this (remember the Gideon of Judges 6)?*
> ❓ *What do the Midianite soldiers reveal to Gideon in verses 13-14?*
> ❓ *How does the victory come about?*
> ❓ *What do Gideon and his men actually do (v 21)?*

Go back to 6:12 and remind yourself of what the angel said about Gideon. Looking at the whole of Judges 6 – 7, how have the words of the angel been fulfilled through this weak man?

✓ Apply

As we consider the story of Gideon up to this point, the main lesson is very clear. God is the Saviour—Gideon isn't! God uses a weak and fearful man for his glory and the people's good. Though that lesson is simple to understand, it's very easy to forget in our own lives. We rely too much on ourselves, and think we're the saviour, not God.

> ❓ *How might this be true, for example, as you seek to share your faith with unbelieving friends or family?*
> ❓ *How might this truth that God is the real Saviour help you if you're facing what seems like an impossible situation in your personal life or in your church?*

Take time to pray about those situations and ask for God's help.

To be or not to be king?

Gideon has led God's people to victory. But will his story end well?

The story of Gideon in Judges 6 – 7 has been a story of a weak, fearful man, used by God to save his people from their enemies, the Midianites. The angel said that Gideon was a mighty warrior in 6:12. But we have seen that Gideon is only a mighty warrior because the Lord himself saves his people through him. Judges 8 describes the end of Gideon's reign. Sadly this will be the last time Israel will know a period of peace in this book (8:28). From here it's further decline with a few brief highlights. Chapter 8 shows what happens when one leader makes some bad choices. We need a much better leader than Gideon.

Revenge!

Read Judges 8:1-21

Verses 1-3 show a rare bright spot in this chapter.

- ❷ *How does Gideon exercise wisdom with the Ephraimite complaints (see 6:34-35 and 7:24-25 for the context)?*
- ❷ *How would you describe Gideon's actions in 8:4-17? Compare for example verse 9 and 17.*
- ❷ *Verses 18-19 reveal that the Midianites have killed Gideon's own family. How does Gideon react?*

Will the real Gideon stand up?

Read Judges 8:22-35

- ❷ *What are the people forgetting (v 22)?*
- ❷ *Gideon's answer (v 23) sounds godly, but what do verses 24-27 reveal?*
- ❷ *How do verses 28-35 reinforce this view?*
- ❷ *How would you assess the state of God's people at the end of Gideon's reign?*

TIME OUT

Read Deuteronomy 17:14-20

- ❷ *How does Gideon compare to the laws about the king laid out in here?*

▾ Apply

Gideon's reign leaves us longing for better leadership. And even when God provides Israel with kings, none of them are perfect—even David. We have to wait until King Jesus.

Read Matthew 11:28-30

- ❷ *How do Jesus' claims measure against the leadership of Gideon?*
- ❷ *How do Jesus' words give you strength and encouragement in all the challenges you face at the moment?*

Spend time thanking God for the beautiful qualities of Jesus, our Saviour and King. Ask God to help you trust King Jesus and submit to him.

Unjust rulers

*Most lament psalms focus on the psalmist's difficult situation. This one looks wider.
How do we pray for an unjust world?*

Read Psalm 58:1-5

❓ *Who is the psalmist speaking about, and
what is he saying about them (v 1-2)?*
❓ *How widespread is the problem (v 3)?*
❓ *What image does he use (v 4-5) and
what does it suggest about these people?*

Good government should lead to justice.
However, often those in power are selfish
and unjust. In human terms there is little
that most of us can do about unjust leaders.
But there is always one thing that God's
people can do. They can pray to the Ruler of
rulers, who is just and calls those who rule
under him to be just.

···· TIME OUT ································

Some translations have "rulers" in verse 1.
Others have "gods". In the psalmist's world
many nations saw their kings as similar to
gods—both of them very powerful beings
that could do what they liked. In some
countries in our world, people will still feel
like this.

Read Psalm 58:6-11

❓ *What does the psalmist ask God to do
(v 6-8)?*
❓ *What will be the response to this
(v 9-11)?*

There are some difficult images in these
verses. How can we make sense of them?
We need to remember that this is a prayer

about injustice. We may be reading it while
living in relative comfort and in a country
where the justice system works reasonably
well. If so, it invites us to identify with the
oppressed, and to join their passionate call
for justice. For example:

- Breaking the teeth (v 6) of predators who
attack prey means freeing the prey (in
their mouths)—thus removing the weapons of the unjust powers.

- Washing feet in blood (v 10) is not an
image of bathing but of victory in battle.
(The victorious side walk through the
blood-soaked battleground.)

Verses 6-11 are a series of images calling
on God to fight injustice. It is based on the
faith that he is the just, supreme Ruler who
can act and beat the mighty unjust powers.

⌄ Apply

❓ *Do you believe—really believe—that
God can act against any injustice and
any powers on Earth?*
❓ *Do you therefore pray earnestly for this
to happen?*

⌃ Pray

Think of the wider world. Choose one or
two places where unjust rulers are oppress-
ing people. Bring them before God and ask
him to act— to break their "teeth" and free
their "prey".

The thornbush king

What kind of ruler do you want to rule you? What kind of leader do you want? What factors shape your decision when it comes around to voting?

Gideon started weak and fearful, but became a strong and faithful leader. But then he acted like a king, hoarding wealth, taking many wives, and behaving ruthlessly. The result was a nation that forsook God (8:27). Chapter 9 sees the continuing slide downwards of the people under a "king" who is a disaster. How we need a better president, prime minister or king than Abimelek!

A leader after our own hearts

Read Judges 9:1-21

- ❷ How does Gideon's son promote himself to his family in verses 1-3?
- ❷ How do the people choose this leader?
- ❷ What do verses 4-6 reveal about his true character?
- ❷ Jotham, the youngest of Gideon's sons, survives. What does his story in verses 7-15 prophesy about the "reign" of Abimelek?
- ❷ How does he apply the story in v 16-20?

Notice where Jotham lays the responsibility for Abimelek's kingship—verses 16 and 18.

☑ Apply

It's said that we get the leaders we deserve.

- ❷ What kind of leaders do you really long for in your country and in your church?
- ❷ But how do our sinful attitudes obstruct

these desires when it comes to actually choosing leaders?
- ❷ *How might this story help us think more biblically about how to choose leaders and what qualities we seek in them?*

TIME OUT

Look up 1 **Timothy 3:1-7** to see the qualities God requires in church leaders.

- ❷ *How different are these qualities to Abimelek's?*

From bad to worse

Read Judges 9:22-57

- ❷ *What are the key events in this section— who rebels and how does Abimelek respond?*
- ❷ *How is Abimelek acting like a Canaanite oppressor of God's people (v 45, and compare 4:2-3 with 6:4-6)?*
- ❷ *What is God's role in this, and why is that significant (9:23-24 and 56-57)?*

☑ Apply

All this is grim news for God's people. They reject God, appoint a bad leader and suffer the consequences. God is there, but only in judgment. It all points again to the need for godly leadership that only Jesus can provide. Turn Philippians 2:5-11 into praise for Jesus and pray that your own church leaders would follow Jesus' example.

A foolish vow

Is there any hope when life is complicated and messy? Judges 9 saw a new low for the people of God. Can things get worse? Sadly they can, and they will.

The story of Jephthah is another step down. Judges doesn't simply go round in circles. It's a downward spiral into ever-deepening brokenness and sin. But even in these dark chapters, there is hope and light.

Light in the darkness?
Read Judges 10:6 – 11:11

The familiar cycle of Judges happens again.

- ❷ *Why do you think God challenges the people as he does in 10:14?*
- ❷ *What hints are there in verses 15-16 that the people have understood the key issue?*
- ❷ *In what ways is God's response at the end of verse 16 a glimmer of hope?*
- ❷ *How is the people's treatment of God reflected in the way they treat Jephthah?*

✓ Apply

In some ways, our treatment of God's leaders often mirrors our treatment of God.

- ❷ *Why do you think this is?*

10:16 sees the people breaking with their false gods and idols. Idols are anything or anyone that replaces God at the centre of our hearts.

- ❷ *What idols can you identify in your own heart that you know you struggle with?*
- ❷ *What steps can you take to loosen their grip on you and get rid of them?*

Read Judges 11:12-28

These verses show Jephthah acting wisely in the face of provocation.

- ❷ *How is his wisdom with the Ammonites shown?*
- ❷ *What do you make of the fact that people like Gideon and Jephthah can act so wisely but also so foolishly?*
- ❷ *Does this encourage you as you think about your own heart and mind?*

A tragic end
Read Judges 11:29 – 12:15

- ❷ *How does Jephthah act foolishly with his vow (11:30-31, 34-35) and with his own people (12:1-6)?*

Child sacrifice was forbidden in Israel. Jephthah could have sought forgiveness and offered an animal sacrifice instead (see Leviticus 27:1-4).

- ❷ *What does Jephthah's vow reveal about his heart towards God and his law?*

This is a very dark chapter. But God still graciously uses a sinful man to rescue his repentant people (Judges 11:32).

Think of those you know going through difficult times. Pray that they would trust in the Lord who brings light and rescue even in the darkest moments.

A fresh start?

If you were drawing up the qualities needed in a saviour, what would you include?

Looking back through all the judges we've studied so far, we've seen amazing strengths and pitiful weaknesses in the saviours of God's people. There have been some staggering highs, but also some deeply depressing lows. And it appears things are getting worse. But now, a new saviour arises whose story is very different. Samson is given more chapters than any other judge, and his birth is told in some detail in chapter 13.

Read Judges 13:1-5

- ❷ *Verse 1 describes the familiar cycle, but what is missing?*
- ❷ *How does this highlight God's grace in what follows?*
- ❷ *How does Manoah's situation in verse 2 reflect the spiritual state of the nation at this time?*
- ❷ *What does the angel promise in verses 3-5?*
- ❷ *How does this promise get to the heart of the big issues in this family's and the nation's lives?*

···· **TIME OUT** ··

Read Numbers 6:1-8

- ❷ *What is the point of the Nazirite vow?*
- ❷ *What is different in Samson's case and how does this highlight how special he is (see Judges 13:5)?*

Faithlessness and mercy

Read Judges 13:6-25

These verses describe the response of Manoah to the news his wife receives. He prays that the angel would come back and then God answers the prayer.

- ❷ *What new information, if any, does Manoah receive?*
- ❷ *What does the story reveal about Manoah's heart?*
- ❷ *What does the story show us about God's faithfulness, grace and mercy?*

This remarkable story feels like a fresh start in a dark book. Perhaps this time, the promised saviour will deal with Israel's heart issues once and for all! But the story also points us forward to another childless woman, who is spoken to by an angel.

Read Luke 1:26-38

- ❷ *What differences and similarities do you notice between Mary's story and Judges 13?*
- ❷ *What gives us confidence that the child of Luke 1 is a better Saviour than the child in Judges 13?*

Both Manoah and Mary had to believe the word of God. The challenge for us is to do the same.

- ❷ *In what ways might you disbelieve God's word that Jesus is the perfect Saviour for you?*

Goes off script

Samson's life seems more like a Hollywood film script than a story in the Bible. But even here, God is at work!

Judges 13 felt like a fresh start. A boy was born who we're told would "take the lead in delivering Israel from the hands of the Philistines" (13:5). At the end of the chapter, the Spirit was already stirring him (13:25). But in order to be the rescuer God wanted, he was set apart from birth to be holy. His parents were to treat him as a Nazirite, one devoted to the Lord. His hair would never be cut, he could not drink alcohol, and he should never touch dead bodies. He was to be a holy saviour. How does he get on?

Not so holy!
Read Judges 14:1-20

❓ *What does Samson's choice of wife reveal about his heart (v 1-3)?*

Remember how the people themselves acted in Judges 3:5-6.

❓ *How do Samson's actions in 14:5-10 undermine his Nazirite vow (the word for "feast" in verse 10 implies alcohol)?*

Samson sets his groomsmen a riddle (v 12-13) with the loser giving 30 sets of clothes to the other. An expensive wager! However, in the culture, Samson should have given his groomsmen the clothes as a gift. His riddle, which they could never work out, was a ruse to get out of giving the gift.

❓ *What are the results of Samson's greed in verses 12-20? Notice verses 15 and 19.*

✅ Apply

Samson's actions here are far from holy; quite the opposite in fact. But in many ways, he reflects what is happening in the nation as a whole. He is blindly following ungodly desires, and ignoring the Lord and his calling.

❓ *Why is holiness important for God's people (see 1 Peter 1:14-16)?*
❓ *In what areas of your life can you see yourself being attracted more to unholiness than holiness? Perhaps, like Samson, something you look at, something you desire, or allowing anger to fester and blow up?*

A cycle of revenge
Read Judges 15:1-20

❓ *How does revenge and vendetta work out in this chapter?*
❓ *What are the consequences?*

Like many chapters in Judges, these chapters are gory and dark.

❓ *But can you see God's hand in any of this? See for example 14:4, 6, 19; 15:14-15, 18-19.*
❓ *What does this teach us about God's commitment to his people, and his power to bring good out of evil?*

A glorious ending?

The story of Samson and Delilah is one of the most memorable in Judges. But it's less about love and more about grace!

Samson's rule as judge has lasted 20 years (15:20; 16:31). But in that time, he's acted less like the godly saviour he was meant to be and more like the Philistines he was sent to destroy. His track record hasn't been great. He's more interested in sex, revenge, money and an easy life. He's seemed very uninterested in pursuing the mission God has given him (see 13:5); even though he has great Spirit-given power to rip a lion to pieces, capture 300 foxes and kill numerous Philistines with a donkey's jawbone. As the worst of the judges, Samson is a very odd choice for a saviour—but through it all God's grace shines bright to point us to a better Saviour.

When godliness is in second place
Read Judges 16:1-22

- ❓ *In verse 1, what do we learn about Samson's time in Philistine Gaza?*
- ❓ *How does he use his powers in verse 3? What should he have been doing (13:5)?*
- ❓ *What does all this reveal about his heart and desire to do God's work?*
- ❓ *Why do you think Samson doesn't just walk away when he discovers Delilah's duplicity?*

✔ Apply

We're more like Samson than we perhaps care to admit. We follow our passions and they lead us into trouble. But we think we can deal with it all with our own strength, intelligence, skills or money.

- ❓ *Have you ever fallen into this trap?*
- ❓ *What steps can you take to make sure you don't fall for such temptations?*

Deeply flawed saviour
Read Judges 16:23-31

The Philistines have their prize and celebrate with their god.

- ❓ *What is the attitude behind Samson's prayer in verse 28?*
- ❓ *How good a saviour was he, given the author's comment in verse 30?*

✔ Apply

The story of Samson probably leaves us with more questions than answers. At best he's deeply flawed, his motives sinful, and his results mixed. But...

Read Hebrews 11:32-34; 12:1-3

As flawed as the four men mentioned in verse 32 were, they are still described as "men of faith". This gives us hope as equally flawed believers.

Ask God to give you courage to press on in faith, despite your failings, fixing your eyes on Jesus, your Saviour.

The land with no king

If no one's in charge, then we can make up the rules. Many people dream of a world like that. And yet the reality is often far removed from what people think it would be.

"In those days Israel had no king; everyone did as they saw fit" (17:6). That phrase comes twice in today's passage (also 18:1) and then twice more in the final chapters of Judges (19:1 and 21:25). It's a phrase that really sums up what is happening in the final chapters of Judges. The last judge in the book, Samson, was an utter disaster—even though God was merciful and gracious. But now the restraints are coming off. Chapters 17 – 21 are some of the darkest chapters in the whole Bible. They show us what happens when human beings ignore God and put themselves on the throne in their lives—the result is chaos and carnage. There are very few references to God in these chapters. How we need a perfect King to rule us...

Do-it-yourself religion
Read Judges 17:1-13

- ❷ How does Micah relate to God in this chapter?
- ❷ What do you think he's trying to do to God (verse 13)?
- ❷ How is verse 6 a commentary on the whole chapter?

☑ Apply

Look up Deuteronomy 4:15-16, 25-26; 12:4-6, 8.

- ❷ How much does Micah get wrong?

- ❷ What will happen if you conduct your relationship with God on your own terms and for your own comfort?
- ❷ In what ways do you try and barter with God to get his blessing?

Do-it-yourself morality
Read Judges 18:1-31

We met the Danites in 1:34. They failed to take the land allotted to them, and now that failure comes back to haunt them. They need to find new land.

- ❷ How do the Danites try and justify their actions (see 18:5-6, 10)?
- ❷ What do we discover about the Levite's motives in verses 18-20?
- ❷ Why is Micah's comment in verse 24 so sad?
- ❷ The story ends with the Danites in their newly conquered city. What do verses 29-30 reveal about their hearts?

☑ Apply

- ❷ How do these chapters warn us about thinking that success in what we do is a sign of blessing?
- ❷ What do they show us about the dangers of ignoring God's word?

Wake-up call

Do you ever feel that God isn't paying attention to you and your needs? If so, how do you pray to him? This psalm gives you an example.

Read Psalm 59:1-17

- ❓ *How does the psalmist describe those against him (v 1-7)?*
- ❓ *Does he deserve what is happening (v 3-4)?*
- ❓ *What does he ask God to do (v 1, 5, 10-13)?*
- ❓ *What are the differences between the repeated sections (v 6-10 and 14-17)?*

Dogs and God

The psalmist is being attacked by people he describes as wild dogs prowling around (v 6, 14). In David's time and culture, dogs were not pets, but rather dangerous, wild scavengers. (We might say jackals or wolves.) They are bold to attack, thinking that nobody is listening, nobody will stop them (v 7). But the psalmist knows some-one who is listening—his God.

- ❓ *How does he describe God (v 1, 5, 8-10)?*
- ❓ *What does he want God to do (v 1-2, 4-5)?*

The words of verses 4-5 are shocking. He asks God to rouse himself (literally "wake up!"). Does this suggest that God isn't watching, or that God is somehow asleep?

And yet at the same time he describes God as his fortress, someone to rely on (v 9-10, 16-17). Sleepy watchmen aren't reliable! How do we understand this?

This is lament, spoken in faith. The psalmist knows, loves and trusts God. Yet his current situation doesn't seem to match his faith. It looks to him as if God isn't watch-ing, because of his troubles. But then note his response. He doesn't just ignore God, but rather calls out to him. It is because he trusts that God is reliable that he can call on him to act and show himself relevant to the situation.

We might be shocked by the words he uses, but he is talking to his heavenly Father. We can speak to God even more freely than we might speak to our parents, in the freedom of that loving relationship. If we are upset, and in danger of saying something "unfair" to God, he understands. He would rather that we speak to him unfairly than ignore him.

☑ Apply

- ❓ *Do you feel the freedom to tell God to "look" or "wake up!" if things are very difficult?*

This psalm gives you that freedom.

⌃ Pray

Bring your needs and frustrations before your loving heavenly Father. Don't worry about offending him. Honesty comes first.

Heart of darkness

Think of some of the stories in the news at the moment. What sorts of things are human beings capable of?

We're in the final dark chapters of Judges. This chapter starts with the refrain, "In those days Israel had no king". The result is that everyone makes up their own religion, (chapter 17) and their own rules (chapter 18). If we thought things couldn't get worse, it does. It's a deeply sobering chapter and there's no avoiding how horrific it is.

One dreadful night

Read Judges 19:1-30

Verses 1-10 tell of a relationship breakdown and an attempted reconciliation.

- ❷ *What picture do we get of the woman's father?*
- ❷ *How does this contrast with the people of Gibeah in verse 15?*
- ❷ *In what follows, how is the woman treated by the old man, by the Levite and then by the men of the town?*
- ❷ *What do you think is the Levite's intention by his actions in verse 29?*
- ❷ *What does the comment in verse 30 reveal about the state of the nation at this time?*

☑ Apply

The tragic truth about this passage is that God's people (the men of Gibeah) have acted like the Canaanites that the Levite tried to avoid in Jebus. God's people are the ones acting abominably towards the woman.

They have become like the nations around them. While this chapter is extreme, it is a deeply sobering warning of what happens when God's people take on the morals of the culture around them.

- ❷ *In what ways are believers today in your culture in danger of taking on the values and morals of the non-Christian world?*
- ❷ *In what ways can you see this happening in your own heart?*

Déjà vu?

Genesis 19 relates a very similar story of how Lot and his family were trapped in Sodom. Sodom is used in the Bible as an example of extreme ungodliness. Sadly, in Judges, there are no angels to save the day.

- ❷ *Why do you think Scripture contains such horrific accounts? What do these stories teach us about the human heart?*
- ❷ *What does it remind you about your own heart?*

☑ Pray

Spend some time confessing your own sin to the Lord. Thank him that though our hearts are dark, there really is forgiveness in Jesus.

When the cavalry came

When bad things happen in our world, we all long for justice. Justice is a good thing, until it finally arrives with us. And then we can discover it has a bitter after-taste.

We last saw Israel reeling from the horrors of chapter 19. A woman has been systematically abused and then murdered. Not by Canaanite enemies, but by God's own people! What is going to happen next?

United front

Read Judges 20:1-25

Israel are finally united for the first time in the book of Judges. What Deborah, Gideon and Samson couldn't do, the Levite does with his grim story (v 1-2, 8, 11). But they unite against one of their own tribes, the Benjaminites, who were the culprits of the hideous crime in Gibeah. The battle is very like chapter 1 (compare 1:1-2 with 20:18, for instance) but the enemy is their brother!

- ❓ *How does the Levite's story in verses 4-7 differ from what happened?*
- ❓ *How does the change of details obscure his own sin in the affair (see 19:22, 25)?*
- ❓ *Why do you think the Benjaminites did not listen to the rest of the Israelites in 20:12-13?*
- ❓ *What does this reveal about the fragile state of the nation?*
- ❓ *What happens in verses 14-25?*

Judgment executed

Read Judges 20:26-48

So far, Israel has faced stiff opposition from the Benjaminites. But now the battle turns.

- ❓ *What good thing does Israel do in verses 26-28?*
- ❓ *How is the victory achieved in verses 29-48?*

The Israelites have their vengeance. But it comes at great cost. Thousands of Israelites lie dead, and the nation is fractured.

- ❓ *What is God's role in all this (v 18, 23, 28, 35)?*
- ❓ *Why do you think he allowed Israel to be defeated twice before their victory?*

⌄ Apply

Israel seeks justice, but pays a heavy price. The woman's death is avenged, but it's been a bloodbath, and justice has turned into a vendetta (v 48). It's a reminder that no one is without sin. We long for justice in our world, but we have to understand that our own hearts need dealing with too.

Read 1 Peter 2:21-25

- ❓ *How does Jesus' example help us when wronged?*
- ❓ *How does his death enable us to begin to find peace and healing when wronged?*

⌃ Pray

Spend some time confessing your own sin before the Lord. Ask God for grace to deal with injustice, and to be able to leave it with him.

A messy end

The book of Judges ends with a messy solution to a self-inflicted problem. Can there be any hope?

The last two chapters have been a grim read. The whole story speaks of the decay of the nation of Israel, and a people doing what they want because there is no king to rule them. But we've also seen, if only they could see it, that there is a King—God himself. But they fail to listen to his word and do what he says. The result is chaos. Now as the book ends, the Israelites try and sort out the problem they have created with a worse solution!

Adding fuel to the fire

Read Judges 21:1-12

The civil war between the Benjaminites and the rest of Israel was a bloodthirsty affair. It ended with the virtual annihilation of Benjamin, with only 600 men remaining (20:47-48). To make things worse, Israel had made a vow not to allow their daughters to marry any remaining Benjaminites (21:1, 7). With the tribe almost wiped out, there was now no way for the remnant of the tribe to survive—there were no women through whom children could be born.

> ❓ *What is Israel's emotional response to the events of chapter 20?*
> ❓ *How do they try to resolve the problem (21:10-12)?*
> ❓ *In what ways are Israel's actions less about justice and more about finding a way out of their problem?*

Back where we started, but worse

Read Judges 21:13-25

When the women from Jabesh Gilead are counted up, there are only 400. Two hundred short for the 600 Benjaminites.

> ❓ *How does Israel sort this problem out?*
> ❓ *Given this whole sorry saga began with the horrific treatment of the woman in chapter 19, how is this ending to the story sadly ironic?*
> ❓ *What does all this reveal about the hearts of the people of Israel?*
> ❓ *What is God's involvement in this chapter (21:15)?*
> ❓ *How do verses 23-24 offer a glimmer of hope and a sign of God's grace?*

⌄ Apply

> ❓ *How do you feel after reading these chapters and seeing that God's people can do these things to one another?*
> ❓ *What might it reveal about your own heart and motives?*

Spend some time confessing your sin and humbly admitting to God your own weaknesses. Thank God for his forgiveness and grace in Jesus.

And thank God that we do have a King who rules his people with love, truth and perfect justice.

A better hope to come?

The book of Judges ended on a dark note. Thankfully that's not the end of the Bible's story!

Our readings in Judges have covered 300 years of history, and many fascinating individuals. We've looked at remarkable stories like Ehud and Eglon, Deborah, Gideon with his 300 men, Jephthah's dreadful vow, Samson's supernatural strengths and pitiful weaknesses, and then the dark, dark anarchy of chapters 17 – 21. We've moved from the end of Joshua's time, to the time of Samuel and the hunt for a king. This final study gives us an opportunity to reflect on the whole book and then look forward to how the main themes are developed as the Bible's story goes on.

Look back

Read Judges 2:8-19

❓ *How does this passage serve to bring together the main themes of the book?*

❓ *What does it show us about the heart of Israel's problem?*

❓ *What does it show us about the character of God and his attitude to his people?*

❓ *What has been your favourite story in the book and why?*

❓ *What were the good and bad qualities of the judge in that story?*

Look forward

One key problem we've seen in the book is that Israel has no king . Leadership is the big issue. The judges might help for a brief time, but they all ultimately fail. However God has a different long-term plan. The book of Ruth is set in the time of the judges (see Ruth 1:1). But it is a story of hope about how God will provide a new king to rule God's people. From this unlikely foreign woman, and the surprising way she ends up marrying, will come King David. Samuel, who is the last of the judges, prophesies about this king.

Read 2 Samuel 7:11-16

❓ *What will God do through this king?*

Look up

Ultimately, even David will fail. But when we come to the New Testament, we find that Jesus is the perfect King from David's line. He at last will do what the judges failed to do, and what even King David couldn't do.

Read Matthew 1:1, 18-23

❓ *How does Jesus deal with the big unsolved problem for God's people?*

🔺 Pray

Think of one challenge you have faced, one encouragement you have received and one new thing you have learned from Judges, and pray them through before God.

Thank God especially for Jesus, your perfect Saviour, King and God.

EPHESIANS: About a church

Ephesians is about the church. But the way Paul teaches us about church is by setting it in a much bigger story—the story of God's eternal purposes.

The big picture
Read Ephesians 1:9-10

❓ *What is God's ultimate end for human history?*

TIME OUT

❓ *List five ways that the world is not under the rule of Christ. What will it look like for God to unite these things under him?*

Christ didn't come as a conquering king. Instead he came, he lived, he died, he rose again—and he left. This isn't what anyone expected! So how exactly will God accomplish his purpose?

The plan
Read Ephesians 1:1-14

Note all the times Paul uses phrases like "in Christ" and "in him".

❓ *What does God do for people who are in Christ?*

Some day, God will gather up everything in Christ. Until then, God gathers up his *people* in Christ, blessing them under his rule today with the blessings that one day somehow will be universal.

❓ *On what basis does Jesus welcome sinners to himself (v 7)?*

❓ *How must sinners respond to the gospel if they are to receive the blessings of union with Christ (v 12-13)?*

⌄ Apply

Is your hope in Christ alone? Or do you expect your good deeds—like reading this devotional—to count for something? Don't lean on your own merits. Trust Jesus alone.

The present
Read Ephesians 2:19-22

By uniting believers to Christ, God unites believers with each other—the church! God's plan for the end of history has broken into time in the people who are made one in Christ and transformed by the Spirit.

TIME OUT

The last three chapters of Ephesians show us how the gospel changes the way we live.

Read Ephesians 4:1, 17; 5:1, 7, 15; 6:10

❓ *What differences does the gospel make?*

⌃ Pray

Spend a few minutes praising God for his plan to bring everything under Christ and for including you in Christ, to the praise of his glorious grace.

Children of the Father

Family is a blessing—gone wrong. Even the best are deeply flawed. And some are truly tragic.

But no matter how good or bad your earthly dad is or was, there is an ideal Father—and he adopts. This passage tells the story of our adoption.

Choosing children
Read Ephesians 1:3-6

> ❷ *What three divine actions does Paul identify in these verses?*
> ❷ *When did God do this?*
> ❷ *Why did God do this?*

Paul ventured into this controversial territory of predestination for a good reason: to assure you that your salvation does not rest on you. God had been at work long before you were here. And he was at it for the purpose of adopting you as his child.

Becoming children
Read Ephesians 1:5-6

In the first century, daughters did not have the same legal rights as sons. That adds to the splendour of Paul's words. In God's family every believer—male and female—enjoys the full status of a son.

Read Ephesians 1:1-3

> ❷ *God is whose Father, according to...*
> • *v 2?*   • *v 3?*

The beauty of adoption is not just that all believers enjoy equal status with one another. Because of our union with Christ we enjoy the very same status as Jesus. Just pause to appreciate that for a moment. *We enjoy the very same status as Jesus.*

⌃ Pray

Spend a few minutes thanking God for uniting you to Christ and making you his child.

Living as children

Paul identifies two ways in which we live as children of God: submission and imitation.

> ❷ *Read verse 1 again. Why is Paul an apostle?*

⌄ Apply

Rewrite verse 1 with your name and vocation: for example, "Donna, a stay-at-home mother by the will of God". You are where you are by the will of God.

> ❷ *How does (or should) knowing this change the way you go about your responsibilities?*

As children, we should aim to live like our Father.

> ❷ *How can you imitate his love for widows, orphans, and the poor around you? Identify three things you can do to show the love of the Father to them.*

Rejected by God?

Have you ever felt that God was against you, not for you? If so, you are not alone.

Read Psalm 60

❓ *How does the psalmist describe what God has done to his people (v 1-4)?*

❓ *Does this fit with your understanding of God?*

"If God is for us, who can be against us?" But what if it seems that God himself is against us? It is a terrible thought, but that is precisely what the psalmist thinks. The heading to the psalm refers to battles in 2 Samuel 8 and 10. Presumably the people had been defeated and saw this as God being against them. But what do they do? They bring it to God himself.

❓ *What do they ask God to do (v 5)?*

❓ *What does God say in response (v 6-8)?*

···· **TIME OUT** ··

There is a story behind each of these place names that goes back to the conquests of Joshua, when God gave his people the land.

- Shechem and Succoth are places west and east of the Jordan.
- Gilead, Manasseh and Ephraim are Israelite areas, described as God's weapons.
- Moab, Edom and Philistia are non-Israelite areas, described less positively.

But each of these areas is described as something over which God reigns and rules—to do with as he wishes. In blessing or judgment.

After a defeat in battle, Israel recall the promises that God gave about the land and his people. In the confidence of those promises, they call on God to act and help them.

❓ *What do they say about God and victory (v 9-12)?*

Praying in failure

What do we do when our plans for God's work fail? Our temptation might be to haunt ourselves with doubts. Have we done something wrong? Has God rejected our plan or us? Even though, deep down, we know we remain God's "beloved" (v 5, ESV), we can still feel this deeply. The bitter reality of life (v 1-4) is distant from God's promises (v 6-8).

What do we do? We bring it back to God, who keeps his promises. We ask, "Why?" We ask him to help those he loves (v 5). We rely on God, not our human strength, as we know that only through God can we truly succeed (v 9-12). And then we see what God will do, in his time, wisdom and power.

⌃ Pray

Bring before God any failures or setbacks that you or others are experiencing. Then take comfort in the promises that he has given. Rely on his strength to succeed.

Freed for a future

What imprisons people? A lack of education? Income inequality? Dysfunctional families? Poor government? What is the prison from which we must be set free?

Present redemption

Read Ephesians 1:7

The word redemption describes the act of freeing slaves. In Christ, believers have been liberated. But what was the prison?

- ❓ *How does Paul define our redemption in this verse?*
- ❓ *What was the price to purchase believers out of this slavery?*

⌄ Apply

- ❓ *Think about your life apart from Christ. Name five sins that used to imprison you, but which by his blood have been forgiven.*
- ❓ *No doubt there are sins that you still grapple with. What hope do you have that their power has been broken?*

Growing understanding

Read Ephesians 1:8-9

- ❓ *What three things has God lavished on believers (v 7b-8)?*
- ❓ *What (or who) is the centre of God's eternal purpose (v 9)?*

⌃ Pray

Thank God that he has not only redeemed us from the prison of sin but also lavished on us his wisdom, understanding and grace.

Our future hope

Read Ephesians 1:10-12

In the Greek, much of verse 10 is a single, long word that means "to put everything together under one head".

- ❓ *Imagine what the world would look like if it bows to the authority of Christ. How would his unrivalled rule transform our communities; our families; our minds?*

Paul uses a different word for "chosen" from the one in verse 4. This one means "we were claimed as his inheritance". One day everything will be gathered up in Christ, and we who have been blessed in Christ are the foretaste of what will be.

⌄ Apply

- ❓ *How does your certain future need to guide your thoughts and actions when it comes to the uncertainties of today?*

⌃ Pray

Thank God for giving you insight into his will. Praise God for his promise that all will be well for those in Christ.

Ask God for grace to trust him in the midst of any discouragement. Your hope in him is not in vain.

What the Spirit does

The 18th-century writer Samuel Johnson wrote: "Age looks with anger on the temerity of youth, and youth with contempt on the scrupulosity of age".

To put it another way, the older we are, the more cynical we become. Gone are the days of rash behaviour and risky bets. With experience comes bumps and bruises that shake our confidence about ourselves and the world.

This can be a particular problem for Christians. The blessings of Ephesians 1:3-12 sound great—but if they're real, then why is life still so rough? Is the gospel all that it's cracked up to be? Was my confidence in Christ born of "the temerity of youth"? Is Christianity really true?

Paul addresses this problem by directing us to the Holy Spirit.

Giver of light
Read Ephesians 1:13

- ❓ *When were you included in Christ?*
- ❓ *Why does Paul call the gospel "the word of truth" (ESV) instead of simply "the true word", do you think? What's the difference?*

Imprint of ownership

Rulers used seals on documents and objects to communicate at least three things:
- "this item belongs to me" (identification);
- "here's evidence that this belongs to me" (proof);
- "don't tamper with what belongs to me" (safety).

- ❓ *Read Galatians 5:22-23. How does the Spirit work to make believers distinctive from non-Christians?*
- ❓ *Read Galatians 4:6-7. What does the Spirit encourage us to say?*
- ❓ *Read Romans 8:22-23. How does being someone who struggles against sin assure us that we will reach our home in heaven?*

Pledge of completion
Read Ephesians 1:14

The word deposit means "guarantee" or "down payment".

- ❓ *What is a down payment? What does it mean for the Spirit to be a deposit?*

⌃ Pray

Give thanks to God for these three works of his Spirit. Give particular thanks for how you have been encouraged from this passage.

Ask God for grace to recognise the Spirit's work in your life and to enjoy the assurance he provides.

YOU CAN MAKE A <u>REAL DIFFERENCE</u>

Many people are struggling with mental-health conditions, exacerbated by the COVID-19 pandemic and life in our image-conscious culture. But when it comes to helping, it can be tricky to know where to begin, especially if we have very little knowledge of mental illnesses and are afraid of making things worse by saying and doing the wrong things. This wise, compassionate and practical book is written by Steve Midgley, psychiatrist and Executive Director of Biblical Counselling UK, and Helen Thorne, Director of Training and Resources at Biblical Counselling UK. It will help readers understand and respond with biblical wisdom to people who are struggling with their mental health.

thegoodbook.co.uk/mental-health
thegoodbook.com/mental-health

Christian prayer

Virtually everybody prays sometime in their lives. But, as we look at the first of Paul's two prayers in this letter, we'll see that Christian prayer is different, and wonderful.

Knowing God...
Read Ephesians 1:15-17

❷ *What are the two ways in which Paul describes the believers in Ephesus (v 15)?*

Based on verse 15, clearly the Ephesians were not ignorant of the one true God, so that can't be why Paul prays for them to "know him better". It isn't even that they lacked knowing him in their experience, since their faith in Christ produced a love for others. We can go deeper still with God and discover more of his majesty and perfection.

▲ Pray

Paul models two ways to pray for people: thanking God for them and asking God to help them know him better. Take time right now to pray this way for people in your life: family, friends, pastors, teachers, non-believers, neighbours and co-workers.

... through his actions
Read Ephesians 1:18-23

In verses 18-19, Paul identifies three things God has done that, if we understood them, would help us to know him better.

❷ *What are they?*

The first request refers to the expectation we have because God summoned us to himself.

Read Ephesians 3:1-2

❷ *Why can we be confident that God will finish what he began?*

Note that the second request does not speak of God's "inheritance for the saints", but God's "inheritance in the saints" (ESV, 1:18).

❷ *What's the difference, do you think?*

Paul's third request is for God's power to be at work in us (v 19).

❷ *What has God's power achieved (v 19-22)?*
❷ *How does this make Paul's prayer exciting?*

What's on your agenda for today? More importantly, what is God's agenda for you today? What awaits you today may seem to be more than you can handle. Yet Paul says that resurrection power is at work in you.

✔ Apply

❷ *How do you need to pray these three things for yourself today?*
❷ *Who will you pray this for every day this week?*

Saved and created

As you look around, everybody is dead. The businesswoman hurrying to close a deal. The teenager lost in his music. The father holding his daughter's hand. Everyone. Dead.

Yet they carry on: rushing to a meeting, listening to a playlist, walking home for lunch. Is this a horror movie? No. It's your world, right now.

The living dead
Read Ephesians 2:1-3

People not in Christ are "dead" (v 1).

- ❷ *What three sins do "dead" people—everyone not in Christ—commit (v 2-3)?*
- ❷ *Whose direction were you following before conversion (v 2)? How does Paul describe him?*
- ❷ *Where does this approach to life end up (v 3b)?*

···· **TIME OUT** ································

Paul is saying to each of us: *Before you were a Christian, this was you.*

- ❷ *Look back to the time before you put your faith in Christ (if you can remember it). In what specific ways do these verses describe you then?*

Brought to life
Read Ephesians 2:4-7

In his great mercy God did three things on behalf of his people (v 5-6).

- ❷ *What are they?*

❷ *How many times does Paul use the phrase "in/with Christ"?*

⌃ Pray

Take time to praise God for uniting you with Christ, so that his resurrection, his ascension, and his place at the right hand of the Father are yours as well.

Repurposed for good
Read Ephesians 2:8-10

We are not saved by works (v 9). Nothing we do contributes to our salvation in any way.

- ❷ *So what motivates us to do good (v 10)?*

We need to beware two opposite errors. One is that we are saved by what we do (legalism); it leads to pride or anxiety. The other is that it does not matter what we do (license); it leads to laziness or immorality. The gospel tells us we are God's handiwork, saved by grace, created for good works.

⌄ Apply

- ❷ *When do you find it most attractive to think that your good works save you?*
- ❷ *When do you find yourself thinking that your good works don't matter?*
- ❷ *How will the gospel make a difference?*

Gospel numbers

A common gospel illustration is of a guy on one side of a great divide, who cannot cross over to God. But the cross has bridged the gap, and it brings him to God.

That's a beautiful picture of the gospel. But it's lacking something that is right at the heart of the gospel message.

Two

Read Ephesians 2:11-12

❓ *Paul describes people who were not part of Israel in five ways (v 12). What are they?*

Before Jesus came and lived and died, Israel were God's chosen people. To be born as a Gentile meant to be born outside of God's people.

❓ *Which of those descriptions point to our separateness from God?*
❓ *Which point to our separateness from God's people?*

One

Read Ephesians 2:13-16

Unlike the "far away" Gentiles, Israel were "near" because of God's promises.

❓ *What has Christ accomplished for these two groups (v 14-16)? (Hint: Paul gives three different answers.)*
❓ *How does Paul make the point that the cross is what unites Jews and Gentiles?*
❓ *So what achievement of Jesus' death is Paul focusing on here?*

☑ Apply

Paul says that Jesus put "hostility" to death (v 16).

❓ *Are there any brothers or sisters in your church towards whom you are hostile? What is the source of that hostility? How does your hostility reflect a low view of Christ's death?*
❓ *What would change in your attitude towards that person if you remembered Paul's teaching here?*

Three

Read Ephesians 2:17-18

❓ *What role does each member of the Trinity have in our salvation?*

That opening picture of the gospel isn't wrong, but it is incomplete. For on the other side of the cross is not just God, but God and his people. Nearness to God necessarily includes nearness to his children.

And what bridges the divide is not only the cross of the Son. It is also the Spirit, who gives us faith in the Son's death for us. The Son's death and the Spirit's work bring us to the Father—whether we are Jew or Gentile, rich or poor, black or white. We are all equally in need of the cross, and are all equally saved through faith in Christ. *Thank God now not only for saving you but for saving you to be part of his united people.*

Welcome to my house

"House" is the key word today. In four verses, Paul uses the Greek root for house five times—"household", "built", "building", "built", "dwelling"—in three different ways.

Family

Read Ephesians 2:19-20

The contrast between "foreigners" and "fellow citizens" recalls verses 11-18, where those who were far from God are brought near to God and his people by means of the cross. That's when Paul introduces the picture of a house—specifically, a household.

···· TIME OUT ····

❷ *What does the image of a family contribute to our understanding of the relationship believers have with one another?*
❷ *How is it both exciting and challenging?*

The "apostles and prophets" refer to the men and women of the first generation of Christians who carried the gospel far and wide, planting churches as they did so. Their teaching is found in our New Testament; our churches are the descendants of the ones they founded.

❷ *So what does it mean for us today to be "founded" on their work?*

Temple

Read Ephesians 2:21

❷ *Read 2 Chronicles 7:11-22. What was the purpose of the Old Testament temple?*
❷ *Read John 2:19-21. What was the*

ultimate fulfilment of the Old Testament temple?

⌃ Pray

The words "rises to become" indicate that the church—the people of God—grows over time. Take time to pray that the Spirit would work through your church to bring more people to Christ and to build up those who are in Christ.

Dwelling

Read Ephesians 2:22

We can (and should!) rejoice that some day we will dwell in the house of the Lord for ever (Psalm 23:6). But we also need to remember and rejoice in the truth that right now God is dwelling in his people. His "house" is—us.

⌄ Apply

The Holy Spirit dwells in us, individually and collectively as local churches.

❷ *Think of yourself as a "brick". In what ways are you a fitting dwelling-place for God's Spirit? In what ways do you need to become more pure?*
❷ *Think of your church as a whole. Are there ways in which you can encourage each other to become more holy, like the Spirit who dwells in you?*

Confident king

David is no wimp—he is a hard man. Toughened by years of battle and rough living, his instinct is to make swift, decisive decisions.

He also lives on his wits, having evaded capture many times by his cunning. He was able to handle a vicious lion, a marauding army or the subtlest plot against him. Virtually anyone with these qualities and abilities would be proud, confident and self-assured.

Humble king

Read Psalm 61

❷ *What is David's basic attitude—where does his confidence lie?*
❷ *What clues do we have to David's current predicament (v 1-2 and 4)?*
❷ *What does he see as his greatest need in this time of trial (v 2 and 7)?*

In a faraway place (v 2), David pours out his troubled heart to the Lord and in doing so, he reveals one of the most fundamental truths that a human being needs to know— that our only hope is in God.

⌄ Apply

There is a great temptation to think that as we mature as Christians, we should become increasingly able to cope with whatever life throws at us. But real Christian maturity is a mindset that says, "I can do absolutely nothing in my own strength". A sign of Christian growth is our recognition that the only safe place to be is in our God, who is our refuge and our strong tower (v 3).

❷ *In what areas of your life are you most tempted to rely on your own strength, wisdom or abilities?*

Committed king

David has committed himself to God: he has made vows to him. But he also now lives out those vows daily (v 8).

❷ *Have you ever made a vow before God? What daily evidence is there that you are living them out?*

Exalted King

Read Psalm 61:6-7

David has been promised by God that his line will reign for ever, but not he himself (v 6-7)! No, David is writing prophetically here about the true fulfilment of that promise he received from God. The King from his line who rules for ever is the Lord Jesus. By his faithfulness and loving kindness, he was enthroned for ever before God (v 7). And he is the one who reigns now with faithfulness and steadfast love.

⌃ Pray

And he is the same one who listens now for your prayers and praises. Come to him in humility, to commit yourself to live for him in the sure hope that you will live with him for ever.

Mystery revealed

Every family has secrets. Some are kept from children until adulthood. Others do not come to light until after a parent has died. Every family has them. And so does God's.

Paul is just about to write down his prayer for the Ephesian church (compare verse 1 with verse 14). But before he does, he takes a quick detour (v 2-13) that reveals God's family secret.

Paul knew it

Read Ephesians 3:1-3

In the New Testament, a "mystery" is not some advanced, hidden knowledge that only a few privileged elites may access. It refers to a secret that had been hidden but is now disclosed.

> ❷ *How did Paul come to understand the family secret (v 2-3)?*

How we know it

Read Ephesians 3:4-5

> ❷ *How do we get to understand the mystery (v 4-5)?*
> ❷ *How are we, living in the AD period, in a privileged position (v 5)?*

⌄ Apply

The means by which we grow in spiritual understanding is by reading and understanding God's word (v 4).

> ❷ *How do you/could you make sure that God's word accompanies you through your day?*

> ❷ *Do you remember to pray for understanding?*
> ❷ *Is there someone you could talk to each week about what you've both been reading in God's word?*

What we know

Read Ephesians 3:6

Finally Paul lets the cat out of the bag!

> ❷ *What is the family secret?*

The "mystery of Christ" (v 4) isn't the mystery of who Christ is so much as the revealed secret of what Christ has done.

And it's amazing. The answer to intra-human hostility is not peace accords or demonstrations, but the unity that exists between people—all and any people—who know they are all equally sinners who deserve judgment, and who know that in Christ they are all equally loved and accepted. The gospel breaks down all barriers, because it breaks down our barrier with God.

⌃ Pray

Take time to give praise to God for doing what no one else could do—turn enemies into brothers and sisters.

> ❷ *How can you express this great "mystery" today?*

God's purpose in us

"In any one thing," the pastor John Piper writes, "God is doing a thousand things". Today, we find the Lord working at both the personal and cosmic levels.

Paul's role
Read Ephesians 3:7-9

- **❓** *What characteristics of God emerge in these verses?*
- **❓** *What actions of God does Paul connect with these characteristics?*
- **❓** *How does Paul describe himself? What two works does God give him to do?*

The first word in the NIV's rendering of verse 8 is "although", but this does not appear in the original. So verse 8 could say the exact opposite: not that God gave Paul such a pivotal role *despite* his humility, but *because* of it.

☑ Apply

- **❓** *Do you ever feel that you are too small, powerless or ungifted for the things God asks you to do? How do these verses offer you hope?*

God's purpose
Read Ephesians 3:10-11

While we gain much from Paul's example, the role to which he was called was a one-off; he fulfilled a unique task in the time-transcending plan of God in Christ.

- **❓** *What divine characteristic does God put on display (v 10)?*
- **❓** *How does God display his glory (v 10)?*

- **❓** *Who is the intended audience (v 10)? Who is that, do you think?*

☑ Apply

Verse 10 tells us that when a church gathers together, the spiritual world is watching, and marvelling that God has saved and united these sinners.

- **❓** *How does that excite you about your church, despite all its flaws and issues?*

Our response
Read Ephesians 3:12-13

These verses explore two almost paradoxical responses to God's work in the church. The first is confident access to the Lord.

- **❓** *On what grounds may we approach God freely (v 12)?*
- **❓** *How else does Paul say we should respond to being part of God's work (v 13)?*

We might expect that God's eternal plan would eliminate suffering for his people right now. But Paul's example shows us otherwise. In fact, we learn that suffering for the gospel is for the good of God's people and for his glory.

☑ Apply

- **❓** *Is this your perspective? And is it the perspective you have for your family?*

Prayer and praise

We've reached the end of the first half of Ephesians. We've seen that God has united us with Christ, we're saved by grace, and we're brothers and sisters as church.

In light of all we've seen, what more could we possibly need?!

Prayer

Read Ephesians 3:14-19

Knowledge isn't enough. That's why Paul bends low (v 14-15) and makes three more requests of the Lord (v 16-19).

> ❓ *What is Paul's first request (v 16b)?*
> ❓ *What would result if his request were granted (v 17a)?*

Paul has already told us that God dwells in his people by the Spirit (Ephesians 2:22). So what is he asking for here?! It's that we would enjoy what we already have—that we would experience greater communion with Jesus. It's the difference between someone being in your house, and you sitting down with them and enjoying them being in your house.

> ❓ *What is Paul's second request (v 18a)?*
> ❓ *What is the basis of this request (v 17b)?*
> ❓ *In what two ways would this request be fulfilled (v 18b and v 19a)?*

If the first request seeks power that grants communion with Christ, the second seeks power that grants knowledge of Christ, especially of his love. Again, in one sense we already know his love—anyone who has trusted his death knows that he loves us. But it will take a lifetime—indeed, an eternity—even to begin to grasp how awesome this love is. It is greater, deeper and more wonderful than you or I will ever fully appreciate.

> ❓ *What is Paul's third request (v 19b)?*

The whole prayer moves to this crescendo, an enjoyment of God's fullness that surpasses both our understanding and our experience this side of heaven.

Pray

Take a few minutes to offer all three requests for yourself, and then for every Christian the Spirit brings to mind.

Praise

Read Ephesians 3:20-21

Here we reach the Mont Blanc of the Alpine heights of Ephesians: a praise-prayer to the powerful, wise triune God.

> ❓ *What can God do (v 20)?*
> ❓ *How does this enable us to pray confidently and excitedly?*

Pray

Skim your eyes over the first three chapters of Ephesians. List every truth that is so great that you struggle to get your mind to hold it. Then give praise to the Lord, who has given you all these things, and given you an eternity to appreciate them.

 Bible in a year: Isaiah 45-46 • Mark 11:19-33

How to respond

What should be our first response to all these great truths we've considered? To think about them? To rejoice? To worship God for them? What does Paul think?

Gospel relationships
Read Ephesians 4:1-3

Contrary to what we'd expect, the first response to these truths is not so much God-ward, like meditation and worship, but rather it is relational. In other words, the vertical truths (what God above has done for us below) have immediate implications for our horizontal interaction with others here on Earth.

❷ *What four characteristics does the gospel inspire in us (v 2)? Jot down a few words describing what each one means.*

···· **TIME OUT** ························

The gospel inspires these four in us because they reflect our perfect Saviour.

Read Matthew 11:28-30; Philippians 2:5-8

❷ *How did Christ personify these characteristics?*

·····························

❷ *Who creates unity among God's people (Ephesians 4:3)?*
❷ *What part do we play (v 3a)?*

Apply

Think about your local church. Name three or four specific threats to the unity of your congregation.

❷ *How do the four elements of gospel-shaped relationships (v 2) defuse these threats?*
❷ *What specific steps can you take to defend the unity of the Spirit?*

Gospel oneness
Read Ephesians 4:4-6

The first word of verse 4 is "for", although the NIV does not include it. By saying "for", Paul tells us the reason for his exhortation to humility and unity. And it all has to do with "one".

Almost every "one" in Paul's list points back to the first three chapters.

❷ *How does each "one" motivate us to be completely humble and work for unity?*
  • *"one body" (look at 2:16)*
  • *"one Spirit" (2:22)*
  • *"one hope" (1:12)*
  • *"one Lord" (1:3)*
  • *"one faith" (2:8)*
  • *"one baptism" (see Galatians 3:27)*
  • *"one God and Father" (Ephesians 2:18)*

Pray

True unity is God-given; and it is easily lost by a church, and very hard to recover. Pray for your church now, that it would be more and more united around all these "ones".

Growing up

Ever seen a child with a head that's too big for his body? You don't say anything to his mother—you just hope that, as he grows and matures, his body will catch up.

How does the body of Christ mature, when we members of his body are so immature and our head, the Lord Jesus himself, is so perfect?

Christ gave gifts...
Read Ephesians 4:7-11

In verse 8, Paul quotes Psalm 68:18 as referring to Jesus' ascension and subsequent giving of gifts to his people.

> ❷ *According to Ephesians 4:11, what are these gifts?*

Often the New Testament writers speak of gifts as abilities. But here, Paul speaks of the gifts as people.

⌃ Pray

Take time to thank the Lord Jesus for your pastors and teachers. They are his gifts to you, to enable you to grow.

... to equip the body...
Read Ephesians 4:11-13

> ❷ *What do the people mentioned in verse 11 do with their abilities (v 12a)?*
> ❷ *What happens as this takes place (v 12b)?*

⌄ Apply

> ❷ *How do the leaders of your church equip you for service?*
> ❷ *On a scale of 1 to 10, how open are you to their input? Do you accept that what they do is Christ's way of growing you?*

... so that you mature
Read Ephesians 4:14-16

Now Paul gives three illustrations to help his readers understand Christian maturity: a child (v 14), a boat (v 14), and a body (v 15-16).

> ❷ *According to verse 15, what must we do in order to grow and mature?*

Truth without love isn't truthful, and love without truth isn't loving. Yet our personality may lead us to speak either in black and white terms, or with great affirmation and encouragement, but not often both.

TIME OUT

> ❷ *What is your personality? Are you more likely to speak the truth without love, or not to speak it at all?*

⌄ Apply

Church growth is the whole church's responsibility.

> ❷ *How will you serve your church today?*

Old self, new self

The baseball star just couldn't accept it. Having played for the same club his whole career, he had been traded. Now, for the first time, he faced his former team.

So he donned his old uniform, walked to his old bench, and tried to play with his old team.

Foolish, you say. Indeed it is. His status had changed, no matter how he felt. But it's no more foolish than a Christian living like an unbeliever. And it's all too easy to live as if we're still outside Christ, rather than "in" him.

The old club

Read Ephesians 4:17-19

❷ *What four descriptions does Paul give of the way the Gentiles live (v 19)?*
❷ *What five reasons does Paul give for the way the Gentiles live (v 17b-18)?*

···· **TIME OUT** ·······································

Paul connects a darkened mind, a hardened heart, and sinful actions.

❷ *What is the relationship between these three, do you think? Which one is the cause of the others? Read Christ's words in Mark 7:14-23 for additional help.*

⌄ Apply

❷ *As you think about non-Christian friends or family, do you bear in mind the Bible's description of them in these verses?*
❷ *Why does it matter if you don't?*

⌃ Pray

Our non-Christian friends have a bigger problem than their sinful actions. Their hearts are hardened, just like ours were. And there is only one who can open their hearts to accept the gospel.

Take time to pray for your unbelieving friends by name, that the Spirit would soften their hearts so they would repent and believe the gospel.

The new club

Read Ephesians 4:20-24

"That, however, is not the way of life you learned" (v 20).

❷ *As a consequence of our coming to know Christ, we have learned to do three things (v 22-24). What are they?*

⌄ Apply

❷ *What sinful patterns from your old way of life are ongoing temptations for you?*

Be specific. Take time to name them clearly, and ask God to help you put them away.

❷ *In those areas, what would it look like to put on your new self?*
❷ *What truths about Christ, and who you are in Christ, will you use to motivate yourself to live as a Christian in those areas?*

Contagious confidence

David is again in crisis. But this time it's not his enemies who are causing the pain, it's his supposed friends (v 4). His so-called allies are intent on stabbing him in the back.

Humanly speaking, he has every reason to feel weak and vulnerable (v 3) but there is no hint of despair in his words...

Royal refuge
Read Psalm 62

❓ *How does David describe the character of God (v 1-2, 5-8, 11-12)?*

We have a God who is a holy Judge and a loving Rescuer. Reflect for a moment on God's awesome power and willingness to save.

Royal reliance

❓ *Look at verses 2 and 5-7. How does David respond to God?*

With the truth of God's character firmly in the forefront of his mind, David is able to boldly proclaim that he is secure, even when surrounded by those who hate him. And he encourages others—us!—to think likewise (v 8-10). Ultimately, nothing else—not riches, not people—is worth trusting, says David. Security comes from trusting the Lord alone.

⌄ Apply

Look again at verses 9-10. What are you afraid of? The thought of being attacked by rough criminals, muggers or fraudsters ("lowborn", v 9); or being dragged through the courts by the rich and powerful?

And is verse 10 so very far away from our own thinking? Don't we sometimes think that the way forward is just to cheat and manipulate our way out of things—or else to surround ourselves with the "solid realities" of pensions and property so that we have no need to rely on God?

❓ *What would David say to you loudly and clearly today?*

Royal response
Read Psalm 62:11-12

God has spoken, and for David that settles the matter. He may only have spoken it once, but David hears it twice—in other words, it is God's voice that he will listen to, and not any of the competing voices gabbling in his ears, or whispering in his heart.

❓ *And what is it that he has heard from God?*

Power belongs to God alone. But notice that it is loving power—a love which is strong enough to judge (v 12).

⌃ Pray

Spend some time praising our powerful, loving God. Ask him to help you trust him alone, and say "no" to the alternatives...

How the new self looks

Jesus is unlike anyone who has ever lived. It's no wonder, then, that those who come to know him and follow him become completely different from the people they were.

Liars to truth-tellers

Read Ephesians 4:25-27

❓ *Why does Paul bring up anger in the context of telling the truth, do you think? What is it about anger, even righteous anger, that tempts us to be untruthful?*

☑ Apply

People speak falsely about many things: income, age, weight, political views, relationships, past experiences.

❓ *What areas of your life do you find it easy to lie about? Why?*
❓ *How does finding your confidence and identity in the gospel undermine your motivation to lie in that way?*

Takers to givers

Read Ephesians 4:28

❓ *Paul says it's not enough for a person to stop stealing. What action (or actions) should replace stealing?*

☑ Apply

❓ *Who are the needy around you right now? Name them. What do you have that you can share with them?*

Destroyers to builders

Read Ephesians 4:29

"Unwholesome talk" refers to words that are harmful and destructive instead of constructive, and dispiriting instead of encouraging.

❓ *How does the phrase "according to their needs" (v 29) inform the way we speak with others?*

⌃ Pray

Most of us have certain people who tend to wind us up, so we are especially prone to respond to them with harmful words. Take time to pray for them individually. Ask for grace to speak lovingly to them.

Hardened to responsive

Read Ephesians 4:30; Genesis 6:3-6; Isaiah 63:10; Acts 5:1-11

❓ *How do people grieve the Holy Spirit?*

⌃ Pray

Read Ephesians 4:31-32

Use the six sins in verse 31 as a prayer list to confess, and turn away from every trace of these sins in your heart. Then ask for God's help to grow in the three virtues in verse 32, and to show the same kind of love to others that God has shown you in Christ.

Living like God

Why would a good God send someone to hell? This question keeps many from faith in Christ.

But if you think about goodness long enough, the question turns inside out: how could a good God let anyone into *heaven*?

Sacrifice

Read Ephesians 5:1-2

Here is the answer to our second question.

- ❓ *How are Christians described (v 1)?*
- ❓ *What are we reminded that Christ has done so that we can live with God as our Father for ever (v 2)?*
- ❓ *How do we live out this identity (v 1-2)?*

⬆ Pray

Take time to rejoice that Jesus loved you and gave himself for you. Give praise to God for this offering that atoned for your sins and restored your relationship with him.

Holiness

Read Ephesians 5:3-4

Some tend to limit God's goodness to his loving kindness. But there is another sense to the word good—God is righteous, holy, upright.

- ❓ *How do these verses tell us to live as God's children, imitating him?*

⬇ Apply

Very few (if any) of us can read v 3-4 and not see some of our own sins listed there.

- ❓ *How are you challenged?*
- ❓ *What do you need to ask God to forgive?*
- ❓ *How do you need to change to live as a dearly loved child of God?*

Goodness as justice

Read Ephesians 5:5-7

Since God is holy and just, violating his standards brings punishment—otherwise, he would not be good. An expression of God's goodness is his justice.

- ❓ *What does someone with a verse-5 lifestyle show about themselves?*
- ❓ *What comes to those who are disobedient?*

It is easy to be deceived, or to deceive ourselves, about the seriousness of sexual immorality, impurity and idolatry. It is easy to be persuaded that these things are not always wrong, or that they do not really matter. These verses tell us our Creator's response: they are wrong, and they do matter.

⬆ Pray

Give thanks to God that his Son's death brings forgiveness for any and all sin that we repent of. Pray that you would not be complacent with your own sin. Speak to God about any changes his Spirit is prompting you to make right now.

Bible in a year: Isaiah 62-64 • Mark 14:27-53

Letting the light in

As I write these words, it's noon on an early spring day. The sun is making a welcome appearance—over the next few weeks, its rays will have profound effects.

That's what light does. And that's what the light of the gospel does. It has a profound and far-reaching impact.

Fruitfulness
Read Ephesians 5:8-10

❓ *What change in our status has come about because of our union with Christ ("in the Lord", v 8)?*

❓ *What are we to do in light of this change in status (v 8)?*

❓ *What does our life produce because of this change in status (v 9)?*

🔼 Pray

In God's creative wisdom, he made the sun to be a means of producing life and fruit on Earth. The light of the gospel is to have the same effect in our lives. Pray that the light of his word would illuminate your understanding, so that it would produce this fruit in your life.

Exposure
Read Ephesians 5:11-12

❓ *What two responsibilities do we have with respect to darkness (v 11)?*

❓ *How does someone living in a godly way expose sin that wouldn't otherwise have been noticed as sinful?*

Transformation
Read Ephesians 5:13-14

The light of the sun has a transformative effect on everything it touches. So also our light not only exposes what is there but also causes change.

❓ *What happens to things exposed to the light (v 13)?*

❓ *What effect does the light have on those who awake to its power (v 14)?*

🔽 Apply

❓ *How does this passage encourage you to...*
- *be fruitful in how you live?*
- *expose sin by living in a godly, distinctive way?*
- *seek to transform those around you?*

🔼 Pray

Look through the passage again and pick out the ways in which your identity as a Christian is described. Use them to prompt you to praise God for all he has done for you. And then pray that you would live more in line with that identity today than you did yesterday.

The wise life

We often speak of "the Christian life". There's a big assumption made each time we do—that the gospel should change the way we live.

Throughout the second half of Ephesians, Paul has told us how to live...
- *worthy of the gospel (4:1).*
- *not like those around us who don't have faith (4:17).*
- *with love (5:1-2).*
- *in light (5:8).*

To these he adds another quality: we are to live wisely.

Capitalising
Read Ephesians 5:15-17

❓ *According to Paul, what marks does a wise person display?*

···· TIME OUT ·······································

Paul's words here recall one of Christ's parables.

Read Matthew 25:14-30

❓ *What did the third man do that was so foolish?*

❓ *How do the first two men exemplify what Paul is telling us to do?*

✓ Apply

Write a list of the opportunities that God has set before you and the relationships he has given you.

❓ *How can you wisely capitalise on each one to advance his gospel purposes in the world?*

Controlled
Read Ephesians 5:18-21

❓ *What two influences does Paul mention here?*

Too much alcohol influences our mind and behaviour to the extent of controlling it. Paul wants us to be under the influence— but under the influence of the Spirit, not wine.

Paul offers five results or evidences of the Spirit's influence in our lives (v 18-21).

❓ *What are they?*

✓ Apply

❓ *What do these tell us about...*
- *singing during church services (whether or not we're tuneful!)?*
- *our own times of reading the Bible and praying?*
- *the normality of each day?*

Verse 21 tells us that, since our Lord is Lord over all, believers are to be submissive people.

❓ *How can you do better at submitting to...*
- *state authorities?*
- *the leaders of your church?*
- *fellow Christians?*

What marriage pictures

What do you have if someone is apparently talking about one thing but is in fact speaking of another? A secret that needs explaining. Or a "profound mystery" (v 32).

Read Ephesians 5:22-33

It seems obvious that Paul's main concern in our text is Christian marriage. But in his view, marriage is simply the metaphor pointing to something more, something bigger. To understand marriage, we must understand the mystery to which it points. So we'll take two days to look at this passage: one to consider the mystery and one to consider the metaphor.

Mystery

❷ *What is the mystery to which marriage points (v 32)? What other relationship does that of a wife and husband reflect?*

···**TIME OUT**······································

❷ *How does this truth help us not to make too much of human marriage? Can you think of ways in which we can make this mistake?*

❷ *How does it challenge us not to make too little of human marriage? In what ways does our culture make this mistake?*

Submission

Re-read Ephesians 5:22-24

The word submit means "to arrange oneself under".

❷ *How does (or should) the church arrange itself under Christ's leadership?*

⌄ Apply

Remember, verse 32 tells us that Paul is speaking just as much about our relationship with Christ as he is about a relationship with a spouse.

❷ *Are there ways in which you are not submitting to Christ as your head? What needs to change?*

Sacrifice

Read Ephesians 5:25-30

❷ *What seven verbs does Paul use to describe Christ's relationship with the church?*

❷ *What has Christ done for us? What is he doing for us?*

Paul employs one verb to describe the relationship of the church to Christ, but he uses seven to talk of Christ's relationship with the church.

❷ *What does his emphasis teach you?*

❷ *Which came first: the church's submission to Christ or Christ's love for the church?*

⌃ Pray

Dwell on those seven works of Christ for the church and spend time thanking him for each one.

What marriage is

Now that we've considered the mystery of Christ's relationship to the church, which marriage points to, we're ready to consider what it means for Christian marriage itself.

Read Ephesians 5:22-33

Metaphor

❓ *In what ways is marriage a picture of the relationship of Christ and his people? (Hint: Look for the word "as".)*

Submission

Read Ephesians 5:22-24, 33

❓ *What two verbs describe the way in which a Christian wife is to relate to her husband?*

Remember, the word submit means "to arrange oneself under". This does not mean that wives are inferior or should not think for themselves or should sin if their husband demands it. **Read Genesis 1:27 and Galatians 3:28.** But it is still challenging, and countercultural. It is the husband who is the head of the marriage; he is to bear that responsibility and take that lead, and the wife is to let him.

Sacrifice

Read Ephesians 5:25-33

Paul draws two comparisons for a Christian husband's love for his wife (v 25, 28).

❓ *What are they?*

Remember, Christ loved the church sacrificially *before* we did anything for him.

❓ *How is this a (challenging) word to husbands?*

Yesterday, we picked out the seven verbs Paul uses to describe Christ's relationship with the church.

❓ *What does it mean for husbands to love their wives as Christ loves the church?*

✔ Apply

❓ *If you are a husband... how, specifically, will you love your wife today, and this week, in the way Christ loves his church?*
❓ *Are you leading your wife and household?*
❓ *If you are a wife... how can you lovingly and loyally submit this week? Where do you find that hardest?*
❓ *If you are not married... do you pray for marriages in your church? And do you let Christian marriages point you to Christ's love for you rather than to regret?*

⌃ Pray

Pray for the marriages in your church. Pray for your own marriage, if you are married, and for your role in it.

Then ask God to help all your church's members—single, married, divorced or widowed—to resist the urge to find their identity in their marital status and instead to find it in Christ.

Desert or oasis?

David is in the desert of Judah, on the run from his son, Absalom, who has stolen his throne. He is hungry, humiliated, and in fear for his life and the lives of his close family.

Spiritual desert?

❓ *So how would you be feeling at this moment?*

Read Psalm 63

❓ *Does the tone of this psalm surprise you given his situation?*

❓ *What makes the difference?*

❓ *How does David play with the imagery as he reflects on his relationship with God?*

David isn't taken in by the seeming hopelessness of his physical surroundings. He takes the imagery of the desert, and neatly twists it to talk about the true reality of what is going on. Water is in short supply (v 1), but David remains thirsty for God. He may be living on minimal rations, but David's soul is bloated with the slap-up dinner of God's presence with him (v 5). He and his men may be dropping from exhaustion, but his spirit walks confidently, because he is holding God's hand (v 8).

⌃ Pray

Is it just me, or are Christians today prone to whinge and whine about the things they are struggling with? If we truly believe the gospel of grace, shouldn't we be like Peter and Silas, singing in prison (Acts 16:25)? Shouldn't we be making picnics in the middle of a storm like Paul (Acts 27:33-37)? Shouldn't we be like David, singing for joy and pouring out our thanks to God (Psalm 63: 3, 4, 7)? Why not apologise to the Lord now if you have been guilty of such ingratitude?

The mirage

David is displaying true faith. He believes the promises of God, and not the evidence of his eyes or the blisters on his feet. He knows that, next to the sure realities of God's promise to him, the power of his enemies to harm him is but a mirage that should hold no fear for him.

❓ *What does David look to that convinces him to trust God (v 2, 3, 7)?*

❓ *What should we look to in similar circumstances?*

The sands of time
Read Psalm 63:9-11

❓ *What will happen to those who oppose the Lord's true king?*

❓ *And exactly why will the king's followers be so glad (v 11)?*

What stings the souls of the king's followers is not so much the hardship of oppression, but that lies about the king are allowed to spread unchecked. Those who belong to Jesus should surely feel the same. We can bear anything, but that our Lord should be slandered, his honour impugned, and his majesty mocked.

Children and parents

Parenting is often joyful, but it is rarely easy. We just want the best for our kids. And that's great—but what is "best"?

Just as the gospel completely reshapes the institution of marriage, so it should also direct how we "do" family.

Children

Read Ephesians 6:1-3

> ❷ *What two responsibilities do children have with respect to their parents? What do these mean, do you think?*

Notice that this is "in the Lord" (v 1). A child's primary allegiance and obedience should be to their Saviour, not an earthly parent. But it is "in the Lord" that children find motivation for obeying parents, because they can know that they have all they need in Christ and that Christ has placed them in this particular family.

☑ Apply

> ❷ *Are there ways—at present or, more likely, in the past—in which you've not obeyed these verses? Have you ever confessed to your parents and to God, and repented?*

Parents

Read Ephesians 6:4

Paul specifically directs this command to fathers (although the NIV2011 footnote rightly notes that it can mean "parents"). God's ideal is that every family is led by a father.

This side of heaven, reality is frequently different from that ideal. Many mothers, often through no fault of their own, are the head of their household. The message is the same: don't exasperate; do instruct. The way we bring up our children is meant to show them how wonderful it is to have a heavenly Father. That is what is "best for our kids".

☑ Apply

> ❷ *For parents:*
> - *Think of your children individually. What exasperates them? What do you do that exasperates them?*
> - *What are you doing to instruct them about Jesus and train them to live under his lordship? Do you need to speak to someone in your church about effective ways to do this?*

Our children's salvation does not depend on us. But God does give parents the privilege of bearing the responsibility to teach and show their children the gospel.

> ❷ *Is there anything you need to repent of in this area, either in your present or past parenting?*

☑ Pray

Parents need help! If you're a parent, pray for your own parenting right now. And whether you are or are not, pray that God would show you how you can support parents in your church.

 Bible in a year: Exodus 12–13 • 1 Thessalonians 2

Taking Christ to work

Does the hope of our future in Christ mean everyone should leave their occupation to become pastors or evangelists?

We've seen how the gospel transforms marriage and parenting. Now Paul shows us how it transforms our employment.

Noble workers

Read Ephesians 6:5-8

When we think about slavery, we typically conjure images of the horrific practices of the transatlantic slave trade. But 1st-century slavery was often more like what we might call indentured service—not a far cry from modern employment.

❓ *What five attitudes should mark our service to our earthly employers?*

In verses 5-6, Paul relates this command to Christ in two different ways.

❓ *What are they? How do they affect the way we relate to our employer?*

It is striking that Paul did not tell these indentured servants to try to leave their responsibilities and evangelise full-time.

❓ *What does this teach us about the value of "secular" labour?*

⌄ Apply

❓ *How does this encourage you? If you work, how does your job allow you to show Christ's glory?*

⌃ Pray

Take each of the five attitudes to the Lord in prayer. Allow the Spirit to identify any sinful patterns in how you approach your work, and confess them to the Lord.

Noble masters

Read Ephesians 6:9

❓ *How are employers to treat their workers?*
❓ *What ultimate event provides hope for workers and accountability for masters (v 8)?*

⌄ Apply

There are many areas of life where you may have power over others.

❓ *How could you abuse that power for your own ends? How could you use it to bless others?*
❓ *When are you most tempted to threaten or manipulate others to get what you want from them?*

⌃ Pray

Pray for yourself as appropriate: either as a "worker" or a "master", or both. Pray for those in your church who you know face difficult issues or relationships in their workplaces.

Bible in a year: Exodus 14-15 • 1 Thessalonians 3

On the front line

We've come to the last major section of the letter. And it's time to put our armour on, to stand and to fight.

The warfare

Read Ephesians 6:10-13

> ❓ *Who is our warfare against? Who specifically is not our enemy?*

Christians face opposition all around. This differs depending on our context and culture; at the least, we may face the misunderstanding of government authorities and the sneering rejection of non-Christians around us. But ultimately our conflict is not with them, but with unseen spiritual forces. There is a spiritual battle going on, and every Christian is part of it, whether we like it or not.

> ❓ *What three responsibilities do all believers share in this warfare (v 10, 11)?*

Throughout the letter Paul has emphasised our union with Christ with phrases like "in the Lord" or "in Jesus". Everything we have and need is in him; and all that we do should be motivated by our identity in him. This fight is no different: we are to be (and can only be) "strong in the Lord" (v 10).

And Paul's words at the end of verse 13 help guard us from an unbiblical triumphalism. We aim to stand, not conquer. We win by holding our ground and refusing to give in to temptation or to disbelief.

⌃ Pray

Ask the Spirit to give you the grace of perseverance, to withstand the enemy's attacks and stand firm in Christ.

The weapons

Read Ephesians 6:14-17

> ❓ *What are the six pieces of a Christian's armour?*
> ❓ *What do you think each piece refers to? How it is a defence against the devil?*
> ❓ *What is the only attacking piece of our armour?*

···· TIME OUT ·······

Read Luke 4:1-13

> ❓ *How does Jesus show us how to use "the sword of the Spirit, which is the word of God"?*

⌄ Apply

When we give in to temptation and sin, it is because we have not put on the armour that God has given us.

> ❓ *Think of a sin you find yourself regularly falling into. How would wearing this armour stop you sinning?*
> ❓ *How can you consciously use the word of God in your battle to stand firm today?*

Bible in a year: Exodus 16-18 • 1 Thessalonians 4

Drawing to a close

Sitting in his prison cell, Paul no doubt reflected on his time in Ephesus (Acts 19 – 20): seeing conversions and baptisms, arguing and debating, making a tearful goodbye.

How then to finish a letter to this dear group of people?

Speaking to God
Read Ephesians 6:18-20

❓ *How many different characteristics of prayer do you see in verse 18?*

We often do more talking and thinking about prayer than actual praying. For us then, verse 18 is both freeing and challenging. Look at it again.

❓ *How many times does Paul use a form of the word "all"?*

It's as if he's saying: *It doesn't matter when or where or how you pray. You can pray in the Spirit all the time on every occasion with any kind of prayer. Just pray!*

 Pray

Pray "all kinds of prayers" for "all the Lord's people" in your congregation. And pray for some Christians who you know are "in chains" for their witness to Christ. (If you don't know any specifically, pray for believers in countries where imprisonment is routine for Christians.)

❓ *Why not use your church's directory or address list and work through it over the course of each month, praying short prayers for all the Lord's people?*

Speaking to others
Read Ephesians 6:21-24

❓ *Why does Paul want the Ephesians to know how he is doing (end of v 22)?*
❓ *Why is it encouraging to hear news from other Christians?*

☑ Apply

We can be too slow to talk about ourselves, and what God is doing in our lives.

❓ *Are there blessings, challenges or encouragements in your life that you could share with others, so that they can be encouraged to keep following Christ?*

The end of Ephesians

Take some time to scan-read the whole of the letter, picking out the truths and teachings that have particularly struck you over the last few weeks.

❓ *What three big encouragements are you taking away from this letter? How will you remember them?*
❓ *In what ways has the Spirit been prompting you to change? How will you make sure real change happens in your life?*

Pray

Thank God for all that he's taught you and shown you in this part of his word.

COLOSSIANS: Continue

We're slowing right down to savour a single sentence from Paul—Colossians 2:6-7—that gives precious, powerful insight into how we grow as Christians. But first, the context…

Many choices

Read Colossians 2:1-5

- ❷ *What is Paul's aim in writing to the Colossians (v 2)?*
- ❷ *What is at the heart of all Paul wants to share with them (v 2-3)?*
- ❷ *Why does he think it is so important to write this letter on this theme (v 4-5)?*
- ❷ *Apart from writing the letter, how else is he seeking to help them (v 1)?*

In Paul's absence the Christians in Colossae and Laodicea have fallen prey to alternatives to the gospel being peddled and promoted by others around them. The ancient world had plenty of religious and philosophical ideas on offer. The state religion of the Roman Empire demanded emperor worship, but also many mystery religions—secret societies that offered a pathway to enlightenment, the next life etc. The cult of Mithras, originating in Persia, was one such religion that many Roman soldiers belonged to.

- ❷ *Why does Paul say that Christ is superior to all of these paths (v 2-3)?*

⌄ Apply

The names may have changed, but the challenges to the supremacy of Christ remain in our culture, and even have an influence and draw for Christians.

- ❷ *When and how are you tempted to draw back from the truth that "all the treasures of wisdom and knowledge" are to be found in Christ?*

Attractive alternatives

Read Colossians 2:8-23

- ❷ *What three alternatives to Christ are outlined in verses 8, 16 and 20?*
- ❷ *Where do these false ideas come from (v 8, 18, 22)?*
- ❷ *What ultimate effect do they have on those who follow them (v 8, 18, 23)?*
- ❷ *So why do you think they are so attractive to people?*

We should never underestimate the power that these alternatives have for people. They appeal to our pride. In our heads: when we think we have superior ideas and understanding. In our hearts: when we think that our participation in festivals or events makes us somehow more special. And in our hands: when we think that the things we do—even costly self-discipline—can bring us nearer to God.

- ❷ *So what is it that actually brings us close to God (v 9-15)?*
- ❷ *And how complete is that work?*

⌃ Pray

Ask God to help you grasp how complete, final and thorough your salvation already is if you belong to Christ. And pray that you would see through the fake alternatives.

Receiving Christ Jesus

The Christians were being tempted to abandon the gospel for appealing alternatives. Paul helps them, and us, see how to defend against these corrosive substitutes.

Receiving

Read Colossians 2:6-7

- ❷ *What has happened in the past for the Christians Paul is writing to?*
- ❷ *What ideas or images does the word "receive" conjure up for you?*

There's a big difference between receiving a letter and receiving someone into your home. When you receive a letter, it can be thrown away, filed away, or sit unopened for a while before it is dealt with. You have control over it, and can ignore the contents or respond to them as you wish. The "receiving" Paul is talking about here is more like receiving someone into your home. An invitation that brings immediate responsibilities and consequences. It means trusting them; it means being hospitable to them; it means that there is a new relationship in place that has implications for how you spend your time, your energies, your resources. The same word is used in Matthew 2:13 of Joseph "receiving" Mary as his wife. Becoming a Christian is this kind of receiving.

☑ Apply

- ❷ *Can you remember a time when you purposely "received" Christ like this?*
- ❷ *Are there times when you treat Jesus more like an unwelcome bill through the mail, rather than a treasured and welcome guest?*

Christ Jesus

Paul's point here is that becoming a Christian is not about receiving an idea, adopting some religious practices or committing yourself to a lifestyle as we saw in the alternatives yesterday; it is fundamentally about receiving a *person*. But who that person is leads to enormous consequences.

- ❷ *What does the title "Christ" indicate about the person you have received?*
- ❷ *What does the name "Jesus" indicate about the person you have received?*

We might invite a builder or a neighbour into our home. Perhaps we would run the vacuum around and tidy up the cushions on the couch. But if we heard that the Queen was visiting, there would be much more clearing and cleaning to do! And who Christians have received is the King of Kings. He is God's promised king (Christ, Messiah). He is God's rescuer (Jesus = God saves). Jesus is nothing less than God who lived as a human being, with a human name. The implications of receiving him into the home of our lives are truly staggering.

☐ Pray

Think for a while about who it is that you have received into your life. First and foremost that is an immense and staggering privilege. Express your thoughts to your "houseguest" Christ Jesus.

Comeuppance

Today we have a do-it-yourself Bible study. No statements, no explanations, just a set of questions that will help you listen to God and apply it to yourself. Enjoy!

The complaint

Read Psalm 64:1-6

- ❓ *What is David doing in this psalm (v 1)?*
- ❓ *And what is he asking God to do for him (v 2)?*
- ❓ *Why does he liken words to swords and arrows (v 3-4)?*
- ❓ *What do words have the power to do?*

···· **TIME OUT** ·······································

Read James 3:5-9

- ❓ *Why does God set such a high standard for Christian speech?*
- ❓ *In what ways do you think you need to be more careful with the things you say?*

- ❓ *What is the answer to the "who will see" question in verse 5?*
- ❓ *Is there ever a plan that will never be found out (v 6)?*

Apply

- ❓ *Can you think of times when you have fallen into the same blind pattern of thinking?*
- ❓ *What can we do to stop ourselves slipping in this way?*

The answer

Read Psalm 64:7-10

- ❓ *What do "the wicked" overlook (v 7)?*
- ❓ *What is their inevitable end (v 8)?*
- ❓ *And what is the result on everyone when they see this (v 9)?*

···· **TIME OUT** ·······································

- ❓ *Can you think of some recent examples where this has happened?*
- ❓ *How might we capitalise on this for the sake of the gospel?*

- ❓ *What will all believers do (v 10)?*
- ❓ *What is the fundamental truth that is at the heart of this psalm that leads to such trust and rejoicing?*
- ❓ *Why is this truth such a relief?*
- ❓ *Why is it such a challenge too?*

Pray

- ❓ *What truths about God from this psalm will you praise him for now?*
- ❓ *What will you pray for others?*
- ❓ *What will you pray for yourself?*

As Lord

It's one thing to receive Christ Jesus. But what does it mean to receive Christ Jesus as Lord? It turns out that there is a world of difference.

Moving-in day

Read Colossians 2:6-7

❓ *What difference might there be between receiving Christ Jesus and receiving Christ Jesus as Lord? What do these last two words add to the picture?*

We've been thinking about the idea of receiving a person as a "houseguest"—receiving them into your household. But even if your visitor is a regal one, there is something that does not change. It's still *your* house! They are still present in your living room and kitchen at your invitation, and have no right to order you to do anything.

But if you are a genuine Christian, you have welcomed Christ Jesus *as Lord*. That is, he has entered your life, not as your servant, or even as your equal, but as your master. In a very real sense, you no longer have the right to say what goes. Every aspect of your time, your conduct, your finance and your future is placed under the authority of the Saviour-King Jesus. He is Lord, which means that you are not. You have handed over the keys to the house, together with the deeds, your diary and everything you own.

☑ Apply

❓ *What might happen if someone "asks Jesus into their hearts" but does not understand that they are receiving him as Lord?*

❓ *Did you understand that this was the "deal" when you received Christ?*

Unpacking the boxes

Of course, establishing Christ's Lordship over our lives is something that does not happen in an instant. It takes a lifetime to learn how to live with Christ as Lord. In theological terms, we would say that justification is instant, but sanctification is progressive. We are forgiven for ever as soon as we have received Christ as Lord. But Christian progress is a slow process over time, as we learn to bring new areas of life under his lordship. To shift the metaphor a little, when you move home, there is definitely a "moving-in day", but for many of us, there are unpacked boxes and disordered, or undecorated or properly furnished rooms for many months and years to follow.

Sanctification is the process of applying Christ's Lordship in the various "rooms" of our house. The rooms called "money" and "sex" and "ambition" may remain closed for a while, but one by one, as we grow as believers, Jesus takes possession of these areas of our lives and, by the power of his Spirit, exerts his control over them.

❓ *Do you think this is a good illustration for thinking about your Christian life?*

❓ *Which "rooms" of your life still remain closed to the Lord? How might you start to open the doors?*

Just as… so continue

And so we come to the "secret" of going on, persevering, growing and living the Christian life. And we discover it is no secret at all.

Read Colossians 2:6-7

❓ *So having unpacked the meaning of the words yesterday—what is the "secret" of growing as a Christian?*

❓ *Does that surprise you?*

❓ *Why might it be so important for Christians who are being tempted by "alternative ways" to hear this message?*

❓ *Why might we be tempted to abandon this route to Christian progress?*

The "secret" gospel message that Jesus Christ is Lord is the way we find salvation. And it turns out, says Paul, that it is also the way we *grow* as a Christian. Going on is exactly the same as becoming a Christian— it is to receive and respond to God's chosen King and Saviour, and place ourselves under his Lordship. It has always been tempting to think that there is something else we need. The Colossians were being offered fine-sounding philosophy and special festivals and rituals, and practices of personal discipline as the routes to Christian "maturity. Paul tells us that these things, instead, lead to futility, enslavement and pride.

In our stupidity, we are tempted to think "there *must* be more to it than that!" And yet, each of these alternative ways appeals to our pride. Only the gospel tells us time and time again that we are so utterly helpless that it is by Christ alone, by faith alone, by grace alone, that we can be born again and grow in Christ.

☑ Apply

If you scan the most popular "Christian" paperbacks you will see the same things again and again—fake alternatives of spirituality, arcane religious practices, the newest fashionable ideas, all sold as the latest discovery or the new answer to our sense of weakness as believers. They fail to see that weakness is something that believers who have truly grasped the gospel delight and rejoice in. See how Paul puts it in 2 Corinthians 12:9-10:

> *But he said to me, "My grace is sufficient for you, for my power is made perfect in weakness." Therefore I will boast all the more gladly about my weaknesses, so that Christ's power may rest on me. That is why, for Christ's sake, I delight in weaknesses, in insults, in hardships, in persecutions, in difficulties. For when I am weak, then I am strong.*

❓ *Have you grasped this fundamental truth of the Christian life?*

☒ Pray

Talk to the Lord about the kind of things you are tempted to embrace, rather than the gospel as a route to Christian maturity.

Pray for your church and other Christians you know, that you all would truly delight in your weaknesses, and God's provision of the gospel as their pathway to eternity.

Bible in a year: Exodus 29-30 • James 1

Rooted

Paul now adds two more powerful word pictures to his explanation of God's provision for our growth as believers. The first is thoroughly agricultural.

Read Colossians 2:6-7

- ❓ *What is it that Christians need to be "rooted" in?*
- ❓ *What do you think that means, exactly?*
- ❓ *Why is the image of a tree, or a plant, and its roots, such a powerful picture for the Christian life?*
- ❓ *What are some of the alternative places we could be rooted in?*

Throughout the Bible, time and again, the image of a plant is used to describe what God is doing with his people. We are God's vineyard, where the vines are pruned, pro-tected and nourished. We are a tree that is planted by water. In Jesus' famous parable, the seed grows and flourishes, or fails, depending on where its roots are set.

Roots in the water

Read Psalm 1:1-3

- ❓ *What three benefits are there for the poplar that is planted by the water (v 3)?*
- ❓ *What do you think each of these pictures refers to?*
- ❓ *What is the secret of the sycamore's "success" (v 1-2)?*
- ❓ *What is the reality for those of whom this outstanding oak is the picture?*
- ❓ *Can you see the connections here with our verses from Colossians 2?*

The blessed person of Psalm 1 rejects the popular and cool things that all the other people do (v 1). She isn't interested in going along with the crowd. Rather she delights to think and set her mind on God's word. And the nourishing life-giving water of God's word causes her to be fruitful, prosperous and withstand the hard times of drought. In other words to be resilient.

⌄ Apply

If you're reading this, then you've surely grasped part of what Paul is teaching here. Our roots need to be deep into Christ, and not in anything else. And we access Christ primarily through his word where we read about him. We read about why he was needed, and how we was promised, and how he was born, and all that he said and all that he did. And then the Scriptures move on to show how he was declared to be Lord through his resurrection, and how by his Spirit he exercises his Lordship as people from every race, nation and tribe are called to him as his people. He is the only fertile soil in which we can grow. All the alternatives, no matter how rich, fertile and appealing they look, are poisonous. They will only bring pride and ruin if we base our lives on them.

⌃ Pray

Thank God that, in the Scriptures and by his Spirit, we have access to the Lord.

Built up

The roots (or foundations) are just what is below ground. But what is it that is being built on the visible surface?

Read Colossians 2:6-7

❓ *What is it that Christians need to be "built up" into?*

❓ *What do you think that means, exactly?*

❓ *Why is the image of a building such a powerful picture for the Christian life?*

❓ *What alternative kinds of building could we be becoming—for good or ill?*

As safe as…

When a building's foundations are sound, and when the shape of them is right for what is planned to be built on top of them, the building that rises up will be secure, sound and as the architect designed it. The foundations (or roots) of the Christian life must be built securely on Christ and his saving work. But what kind of building emerges from these foundations as time goes by? Of course, there can be many potential missteps here. And this is something that Paul sees very clearly.

Read 1 Corinthians 3:10-23

The only foundation for a true believer is Christ, but what can be built on top of that can be made of gold, silver and precious stones, or wood, hay and straw.

❓ *What kinds of things do you think Paul means by these images?*

❓ *Can you think of people you know who have built their lives in Christ with precious, valuable things?*

❓ *Can you think of people you know who have built their lives with transient flammable things?*

❓ *What does Paul say will happen at the last day (v 13-14)?*

❓ *What will be the result for both kinds of "builder"?*

⌃ Pray

What a waste! We should be sad at how some Christians get distracted and side-tracked into false avenues of Christian spirituality or service. Some may have the appearance of being good, faithful and noble, and yet it will all be consumed on the last day. And yet, the grace of God is greater than even the foolishness of our deceived hearts. If someone has the secure foundation of Christ, they will still be saved, even though the dilapidated hovel of their lives is shown to be of no eternal value.

Pray for the people you have thought about above. Give thanks for those who are following Christ daily, and seeking to live for him and like him.

And cry to the Lord for those who have somehow got lost along the way. Pray for an opportunity to encourage them to value their foundations, and to start to rebuild themselves according to the Maker's plan.

Just as you were taught

How do we ultimately discern what is good and noble and true? How do we discern which materials to build our lives with?

Read Colossians 2:6-7

> ❷ *Why do we need a teacher in the Christian life?*
> ❷ *In general terms, what makes a good teacher? And what about a bad teacher?*

At my old school there was a much-loved history teacher who spent two years teaching his class about the Tudors and Elizabethans. But when the boys turned over their exam papers, they found questions about the Industrial Revolution. We all love teachers who are passionate, funny, engaged with their subjects and can inspire and excite us—as well as make complex subjects easy to grasp. But irrespective of their character traits and presentation skills, the bottom line is that teachers must teach us the correct things.

Trusted teachers

Read Ephesians 4:11-16

> ❷ *What has Christ given to us to make sure we are built up correctly (v 11)?*
> ❷ *What is the result when we allow ourselves to be shaped by these trusted pastor teachers (v 12-13)?*
> ❷ *What is the character and motivation of those who are not trustworthy in this area (v 14)?*

Good teaching produces Christ-like people. But notice that this whole passage is *plural*. Paul wants us to know that good teaching produces a Christ-like *community* of believers. We might be familiar with people who we consider to be saintly—loving, kind and gentle but truth-speaking and hard-working in the service of the Lord and his people.

> ❷ *But what does a whole church full of people like that look like?*

✔ Apply

> ❷ *How will you contribute to being part of a Christ-like community this weekend?*
> ❷ *False teachers are cunning, crafty, deceitful (v 14). How can we guard ourselves against people and ideas that will appear attractive and appealing on the surface?*

✦ Pray

Pray for those who teach at your church. Ask the Lord to help them remain true to the word of God.

And pray for your church congregation, asking God to help you grow into loving, connected maturity in Christ as you sit under the faithful teaching of your pastors.

Overflowing

We come to the end of Paul's powerful summary of what it means to grow as a Christian believer. What is the sure sign that we are getting all this right?

The heart of it all

Read Colossians 2:6-7

- ❓ *Why is thankfulness at the heart of genuine Christian spirituality?*
- ❓ *Why should it be "overflowing" do you think?*

It's hidden by the English translations, but the word "Thanks" and "Thankfulness" are deeply related to the word for "Grace". It comes out when we offer a prayer of thanks for food, we call it "saying grace". Grace (*charis*) is literally at the heart of thankfulness (*eucharistia*).

If you are a Christian, you are saved by grace. You are sustained by grace, you utterly depend on the grace and loving kindness of the Lord towards you at every moment of your life. Your status, identity, gifts, possessions, relationships and future are all yours because of the grace of God towards you. If you truly understand this, then the only response that is appropriate is for you to be filled with joyful thanksgiving towards God.

Reasons to be thankful

Read Colossians 1:3,12; 3:15,17; 4:2

- ❓ *What aspects of thankfulness does Paul focus on in the rest of his letter to the Colossians?*
- ❓ *Why do you think he needs to underline the need to be thankful so much?*

For one thing, we so easily forget. It's built into our sinful natures to take glory to ourselves. So we need a constant reminder to be thankful, because it makes us focus our eyes on who God is (the generous giver), and who we are (the undeserving recipients). But notice that this gratitude is filled with delighted joy. It's not the polite but begrudging "thank you" that your parents make you say to Aunt Maud when you open her Christmas gift of a weird hand-knitted jumper that will make you the laughing stock of the neighbourhood if you ever wear it. It is the delighted tearful explosion of gratitude when you, a destitute criminal, have been pardoned from a death sentence you knew you deserved, and given a fortune. Expressing our gratitude regularly and repeatedly also serves to reinforce how precious and valuable the gift is that we have received.

✔ Apply

We not only need to express thanks directly to God in prayer but encourage one another in our conversations.

- ❓ *How could you speak encouraging words of thankfulness with other Christians when you meet together?*

▲ Pray

Read the words of Colossians 2:6-7 and turn each word and phrase into grateful prayers.

OBADIAH: Last to first

Do you ever feel angered by how the world views Christ and Christians negatively, and wish that God would turn the tables?

Obadiah is a short prophecy concerning the Edomites, who were the descendants of Jacob's older brother, Esau. God had promised that the older would serve the younger (Genesis 25:23), but it wasn't working out like that in Obadiah's time. Instead, Jacob's descendants (Judah) had been sent into exile by the Babylonians, while the Edomites rejoiced over their brothers' distress.

The heart of Edom
Read Obadiah verses 1-4

- ❓ *What impression do you get of Edom in verses 3-4?*
- ❓ *What hints do we get about what is going to happen next?*

Edom was situated in the rocky area of south-western Jordan where Petra still stands today. The Edomites relied on their strategic advantage for security (v 3). But no matter how high they climb, they will never escape God's reach.

⌄ Apply

- ❓ *In what ways is this same prideful, self-reliant attitude seen in the world today?*
- ❓ *How do you see it in your own heart?*

From nations, leaders, the rich and powerful, down to ordinary people, we all build our lives on our own achievements, forgetting that God gives us everything. He can't let our scorning of him go on for ever.

The consequence for Edom
Read Obadiah verses 5-9

- ❓ *What do thieves and grape-harvesters have in common (v 5)?*
- ❓ *How is this contrasted with what will happen to Edom (v 6)?*

Thieves take only what they can carry, and harvesters skim over some of the crop. But Edom will be left utterly derelict.

- ❓ *What further disaster will befall them (v 7)?*
- ❓ *Edom prided itself on its wisdom and strength. Where does this lead in verses 8-9?*

Everything the Edomites had trusted—allies, military prowess, mental agility—will be taken away from them. It all counts for nothing, as they are totally annihilated.

⌃ Pray

Proverbs 3:5 says, "Trust in the Lord with all your heart and lean not on your own understanding". The Edomites were doing the opposite of this. Ask God to search your heart and show you where you're tempted to be like them.

Then give thanks for Jesus, who was "cut down in the slaughter" (Obadiah 9), destroyed in our place.

A brother's betrayal

Today's passage zones in on the events of the Babylonian conquest of Jerusalem, when God's people were taken into exile (2 Kings 25:8-12).

The crime

There was a lot of water under the bridge for Esau (=Edom) and Jacob (=Judah) but in the face of the Babylonian invasion, we might have expected Esau to stick by Jacob.

Read Obadiah 10-14

> ❷ *How have the Edomites behaved towards their brothers?*
> ❷ *How would you describe their heart-attitude towards Jacob?*

Kicking someone when they're down is bad enough; when it's your brother, it's truly horrific. The Edomites are full of sneering pride and deep hatred, delighted to see Jacob ruined. As he is crushed, their egos inflate (v 12).

☑ Apply

> ❷ *How does this challenge you? When are you tempted to gloat over an "enemy", or even a Christian brother or sister with whom you disagree?*
> ❷ *What heart-attitude does this reveal in you? What truths do you need to remember?*

The cup

Read Obadiah 15-16

> ❷ *What do you think the "day of the Lord" means in verse 15?*
> ❷ *How will it impact Edom?*

In Obadiah 2-15, the "you" is referring to Edom, but in verse 16, this changes—God is now speaking to his own people. Physically, God's people have suffered the terrible loss of their home and nation. But why? What's been going on spiritually? What have they been "drinking" (v 16)? Isaiah 51:17 talks about God's people drinking the cup of his wrath. This exile is happening to them because they've broken the covenant—they've failed to put God first, and turned away from him, and so he must punish them in judgment. But Isaiah 51:22-23 is a wonderful promise: "See, I have taken out of your hand the cup that made you stagger; from that cup, the goblet of my wrath, you will never drink again. I will put it into the hands of your tormentors."

Both drink the cup; both have sinned and must be punished. But whereas for Jacob, the punishment works as discipline and brings restoration, for Edom, the punishment is unending.

Read Matthew 26:39-46

> ❷ *How, ultimately, is God able to restore his people?*

⬆ Pray

Give thanks for Jesus, your faithful brother who drank the cup of God's wrath for you. Pray for the unbelievers God has put on your heart, that they would repent before it's too late, and not face God's continual wrath.

Hope restored

How can we keep trusting God's promise of eternal deliverance when the world around us tells us we're crazy?

Read Obadiah 17-21

❓ *What will happen to Jacob (v 17)?*

❓ *How does this contrast with the people's current situation?*

❓ *How is verse 18 a reversal of what has just happened in verses 10-14?*

❓ *The places listed in v 19-21 encompass the furthest reaches of the promised land. What is the main point here?*

Edom looks strong and Judah/Jacob very weak, but God promises to turn the situation completely on its head—Edom will be utterly destroyed, and Judah restored.

❓ *Why will all of this happen (see the end of v 21 for a clue)?*

It's definitely not because God's people deserve it! Rather, God is revealing his good and gracious plan to one day fill the earth with his glory.

···· **TIME OUT** ···

Read Romans 9:10-12

❓ *What is the point here? How do you feel about it?*

Although Esau is the elder twin, before they're born the promise is made to Jacob (Genesis 25:23). How does that play out? Esau sells his birthright to Jacob for a bowl of stew (Genesis 25:29-34), and then Jacob steals Esau's blessing (Genesis 27). Both are so sinful! Neither deserves God's blessing,

only his curse. But God's choice is based not on our merit but on his mercy.

⌄ Apply

We will reign with Christ in a restored, perfect creation. Not because we deserve it but because of God's abounding mercy.

❓ *Have you really grasped this? Or do you sometimes think God loves you more when you're being "good"?*

❓ *Why is it such good news that it depends wholly on God's mercy?*

We can't lose something we didn't earn in the first place. We mess up, just like the Israelites, but we are eternally secure in Christ, because God cannot break his promise to save us.

As we look at the world around us, Christians can seem very weak, even despised, with unbelievers ruling the roost. How does the book of Obadiah encourage you to keep trusting that God will one day turn this completely on its head?

⌃ Pray

Pray for the world, as nation rises against nation, and God's people are persecuted. Pray that God's kingdom would come in people's hearts, and that we as a worldwide church would remain faithful to our faithful God, trusting that he will one day right every wrong.

LUKE: It is written

One of the most amazing and humbling aspects of the Gospels is that for his whole life, Jesus knew exactly what awaited him at the end of it. He knew, and walked resolutely towards it.

Read Luke 18:31-34

❷ *What will happen (v 32-33)?*
❷ *Where is this already laid out (v 31)?*

The stark facts of what lies ahead are set out in verses 32-33. But to emphasise the significance of those facts, Jesus points us to "everything that is written" about him.

As he told his disciples (for the sixth time in Luke's Gospel) what would happen in Jerusalem, where in the Old Testament was Jesus thinking about? Once he'd reached the city, Jesus pointed people to two particular prophecies...

With the transgressors

"It is written: 'And he was numbered with the transgressors'; and I tell you that this must be fulfilled in me" (Luke 22: 37).

Read Isaiah 52:13 – 53:12

❷ *Which parts of Jesus' prediction in Luke 18:32-33 is this prophecy about?*
❷ *How does Isaiah explain the significance of these events?*

The capstone

"Jesus looked directly at them and asked, 'Then what is the meaning of that which is written: "The stone the builders rejected has become the capstone"?'" (Luke 20:17)

Read Psalm 118:13-24

A capstone is the stone in the centre of an arch on which all the others put their weight, so the structure stays together. Without it, the whole arch collapses!

❷ *Which parts of Jesus' prediction in Luke 18:32-33 is this psalm about?*
❷ *How does Psalm 118 show us the significance of these events?*
❷ *What is the right response to the fulfilment of this prophecy (Psalm 118:15, 24)?*
❷ *How did the disciples react (Luke 18:34)?*

They could not take in the truth that the all-powerful, eternal Son of Man would go through what Isaiah had prophesied. And it would require a supernatural work to enable them to grasp the significance of what happened—it would need Jesus himself to "[open] their minds" for them to understand it (24:45-47).

⌃ Pray

Thank the Lord that he has enabled you to see what he has done for you.

Ask him to keep enabling you to appreciate more and more the truth that he was "numbered with the transgressors" in his death so that you don't need to be; and the glorious resurrection reality that he is the capstone of your life and eternal future.

Blind see, rich give

While those who should understand the King fail to do so (v 34), two more unlikely people enter his kingdom…

....

Read Luke 18:31-34

The disciples don't understand why the Son of Man will die (v 34).

❓ *Could you explain to an interested friend why Jesus came to Earth to die?*

If it's harder than expected, why not grab a Christian friend and practise together?

I want to see

Read Luke 18:35-43

❓ *Compare this man with the man we met in 18:18-23:*
  - *in their social standing and wealth.*
  - *in their emotions at the end of each episode.*

What has made the difference? One man came to Jesus wondering what he could do for Jesus (Luke 18:18)—the other came knowing he needed Jesus to do something for him (Luke 18:41). And that "something" was spiritual healing, as well as physical—"healed" in verse 42 is the Greek word "*sozo*", or "saved". And look how the beggar used his sight. Not to have an easier life but to follow Jesus (v 43), the King who is on his way to rejection and death.

✔ Apply

❓ *Which attitude best describes yours?*
  - *Glad to be saved by Jesus, so you can go to heaven when you die.*
  - *Glad to be saved by Jesus, so that you can follow and serve him.*

Here and now I give

Read Luke 19:1-10

❓ *How much does Zacchaeus want to see Jesus?*
❓ *How does Jesus react to this (v 5)?*

Verse 2 indicates what drove Zacchaeus—money. As chief tax collector he'd given up his reputation, popularity and moral code—for money. Money was what he'd looked to for satisfaction and security in his life, even at the expense of everything else. It was what he'd worshipped.

❓ *Why is verse 8 therefore amazing?*

✔ Apply

❓ *What difference does it make to know Jesus, and look to him to give us what we need?*
❓ *What are the top three things that you find easy to worship instead of Jesus?*
❓ *If you start consistently to look to Jesus in place of those things, how would your actions change?*

▲ Pray

Re-read today's passage and pick out all the ways it reveals to us how wonderful Jesus is. Then praise God for him.

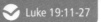

Well done!

The kingdom is coming: so be ready (17:26-37), stay faithful (18:1-8), and—get busy.

Read Luke 19:11-27

> ❓ *What mistaken belief prompted Jesus to tell this parable (v 11)?*

There is going to be a gap between the King coming to Earth to die and rise, and the full and final coming of his kingdom. We, just like the people that day, need to know how to live between Easter Sunday and Jesus' return.

Absent king

> ❓ *Where does the nobleman go, and why (v 12)?*

···· **TIME OUT** ···

The "king" is, of course, Jesus.
Read Philippians 2:5-11

> ❓ *Where is Jesus right now (v 9)?*
> ❓ *How is this wonderfully reassuring?*

Subjects and servants

> ❓ *What do the subjects want (Luke 19:14)? Does this make any difference (v 15)?*

But not everyone rejects his authority. Some of them serve him instead.

> ❓ *What job are they given (v 13)?*
> ❓ *Why is this a great privilege for them?*
> ❓ *How do they respond (v 16-20)?*

The third servant shows he isn't really a servant at all. His excuse in verse 21 is, as the master points out in verse 23, rubbish—if he really did fear his master, he would have made sure he did something with what he'd been given. His actions (or inactions) betray that he thought either that the king wouldn't return, or that while the king was away he'd put his own interests first, not the king's.

Returning king

> ❓ *How does the king respond to...*
> • *the rebellious subjects (v 27)?*
> • *his hard-working servants (v 16-19)?*
> • *the false servant (v 24)?*

Jesus' points are: the kingdom is coming, so don't oppose the King. And the kingdom is coming, so get busy serving the King. The wonderful truth is that when King Jesus returns, he will look at those who have loved and served him with all that he gave them and say: "Well done, my good servant!" An amazing prospect!

☑ Apply

> ❓ *Is serving Jesus a privilege or a duty to you?*

Think about your gifts, your life stage, your relationships, your bank account(s). All are given to you by Jesus.

> ❓ *What would Jesus look at in your life and say to you: "Well done!"*

❤ *Bible in a year: Job 14-16 • 1 Corinthians 6*

The gospel's peak

Luke is a serious historian (Luke 1:1-4)— he is also a brilliant writer and teacher. And this last week, he's been leading us up a mountain and down again.

Foothills: coming kingdom

17:20 – 18:8 see Jesus teaching about how his kingdom will arrive in all its fullness, and how to live in light of that. So the main message of 17:20 – 18:8 is: that the kingdom is coming. *Be ready!*

Read Luke 18:1-8

> ❓ *Again Jesus says that the kingdom is coming. What's the action point for believers (v 8)?*

And we met this theme in yesterday's passage where the message was: *The kingdom is coming. Keep working!*

Higher slopes: into the kingdom

Read 18:15-17

> ❓ *How do people come into the kingdom?*

Those with childlike faith, who simply look to Jesus to provide in life now and life eternally (18:28-30), are in— whether they are blind beggars (18:35-43) or rich taxmen (19:1-10). Next we reach the summit, and we're brought face to face with...

Pinnacle: King of the kingdom

Read Luke 18:31-33

Jesus is the prophesied, suffering, rising King. He's the eternally ruling Son of Man—and he's the suffering Saviour. He's the one who will bring the kingdom in all its fullness, and he's the one who has opened the way into his kingdom. He is the centre of the gospel, our capstone. Our everything.

🔺 Pray

Praise the Son of Man: for what he did in Jerusalem; for making you a part of his kingdom now; and for what he will do when he returns. Ask him to enable you to know him, love him and serve him more today than you did yesterday.

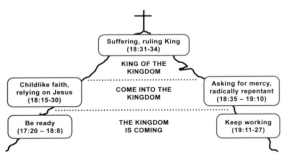

Suffering, ruling King (18:31-34)

KING OF THE KINGDOM

Childlike faith, relying on Jesus (18:15-30)

COME INTO THE KINGDOM

Asking for mercy, radically repentant (18:35 – 19:10)

Be ready (17:20 – 18:8)

THE KINGDOM IS COMING

Keep working (19:11-27)

Sun blessed

Our modern way of life means that most of us are disconnected with the truths contained in this harvest psalm.

Now, food is available all year round, and in abundance and can be delivered to your home at the click of a mouse button. But we need to remind ourselves how much the whole process is dependent upon God.

Blessed

Read Psalm 65:1-4

They may be gathering at the temple ("Zion", v 1-2) to celebrate the harvest, but another matter of greater importance fills David's mind.

> ❓ *What is it (v 3-4)?*
> ❓ *And while they're thinking of harvest feasting, what does David say should really satisfy them (v 4b)?*

🔼 Pray

God forgives! I hope I never lose sight of how astonishing and wonderful that truth is—especially when we consider the kind of people that he forgives (v 2), chooses and draws to himself (v 3)!

Spend some time praising God for this provision of Jesus the bread of life.

Zest

Read Psalm 65:5-8

> ❓ *What aspects of God's character are these verses about?*

> ❓ *What is extraordinary about verse 5?*

David sees that the God of little Israel is, in fact, the God of the whole earth. And also that he is the only hope for the future for the whole planet—even undiscovered people across the farthest seas.

···· **TIME OUT** ························

> ❓ *What does verse 7 remind you of?*

Read Mark 4:35-41 if you need a reminder.

Harvest

Read Psalm 65:9-13

> ❓ *Exactly how is God involved in the world? Trace the details in these verses.*
> ❓ *How generous is God to his world (v 9, 10, 11, 12, etc.)?*

This is all the more remarkable when you realise what we're like (v 3)!

🔼 Pray

God forgives, rescues, rules, provides.

Give thanks for God's physical provision for you in life.

Give thanks that God is the Lord of the whole world. And pray for those you know seeking to spread the gospel message of his forgiveness in other lands.

Coronation march begins

Imagine the pomp of the coronation of Queen Elizabeth II, add the joy of the Platinum Jubilee celebrations, and then with that in mind…

....

Read Luke 19:28-38

- ❓ *How would you describe the general tone of this episode?*
- ❓ *What do these verses tell us about Jesus?*

Lord of the details

- ❓ *What are the disciples told to do (v 30-31)?*
- ❓ *What does verse 32 reveal to us about Jesus?*

⌄ Apply

Jesus is in control. He does not send his followers out into the unknown, but to do the work he has prepared for them. But obeying Jesus can still look risky and terrifying from our point of view!

- ❓ *How does verse 32 encourage you to take risks in following Jesus?*
- ❓ *What difficult thing will you do today if you trust that Jesus knows what he's doing, even when you don't?*

Lord of the heart

The colt is a sign of kingship, the steed of choice for Israel's Old Testament kings (e.g. 1 Kings 1:32-35). As Jesus mounts the donkey and rides into the capital, he's not claiming to be gentle and meek so much as to be royal and ruling.

- ❓ *With what emotion do his followers greet his coronation march (Luke 19:37)?*

⌄ Apply

Take a moment to think about each of these wonderful events, and what each means to you as a follower of the Lord Jesus. Let them thrill your heart. Feel the joy of knowing the incarnate, ruling, risen, heavenly King!

Lord of the cross

The words Jesus' followers choose to praise him with in verse 38 are from Psalm 118. And what they say is prophetic…

Read Psalm 118:26-28

- ❓ *Where does the procession end up (v 27)?*

This coronation march will end at the altar, a place of sacrifice—not in the temple in Jerusalem but at the cross outside its walls. The way to the ultimate coronation at the right hand of the Father must go through the cross, where the King will be sacrificed so that his people might surround his eternal throne.

⌃ Pray

"You are my God, and I will praise you; you are my God, and I will exalt you"
(Psalm 118:28)

Why not do so now?

Peace? No thanks

God's King has come to his city. The highpoint of Jewish history has arrived. The Lord will enter his temple. Jerusalem's people stand ready to welcome and rejoice—or not.

The leaders
Read Luke 19:37-40

> ❓ *In verse 39, how do the Pharisees react to the joy (v 37) and message (v 38) of Jesus' disciples?*

They see the King coming and they say: *No thanks.*

The city
Read Luke 19:41-44

> ❓ *What will happen to the city?*
> ❓ *Why (v 43-44)?*

They see God's King coming and they will say: *No thanks.*

> ❓ *How does Jesus feel about this (v 41)?*

This is the only time that Luke records Jesus weeping. He knows that Jerusalem could have known peace under his rule (v 42). And he knows how horrific the judgment of their rejection will be.

These were not idle words. The events of AD 70, when rebellious Jerusalem was destroyed by the Romans, were far more terrible even than the picture Jesus paints here. And peace has proved elusive since. Jerusalem stands as an example of the folly of being offered peace with Jesus, but choosing destruction without him.

The temple
Read Luke 19:45-46

At the beginning of verse 45, God on Earth enters his house in his city, surrounded by his ancient people. It should be the greatest moment in human history. But it isn't.

> ❓ *What does Jesus do?*
> ❓ *What do Jesus' actions show is his verdict on 1st-century temple worship (v 45)?*
> ❓ *What should the temple be, and what has it become (v 46)?*

God's King sees what Jewish temple religion has become and says: *No thanks.*

The plot
Read Luke 19:47-48

Jesus is a wonderful unifier. He brings people together—in opposition to him. Here, the religious and political elites unite and begin to think what ought to be unthinkable: killing the Christ.

☑ Apply

Rejection of Jesus, even by very religious people, is nothing new.

> ❓ *How does this encourage you to keep living for him even when others reject or despise you for it?*

Toe to toe

The battle lines have been drawn—Jesus Christ v the religious leaders. Today is the first of five verbal skirmishes we'll watch in chapter 20, before the final showdown.

Tell *us*

Read Luke 20:1-8

❷ *What is Jesus doing (v 1)?*
❷ *Why do the leaders interrupt him in verse 2?*
❷ *Why is this, in a way, a fair question?*

Tell *me*

❷ *How does Jesus respond (v 3)?*

···· **TIME OUT** ····························

Read Luke 5:21-23; 10:25-26 (or, if you have time, 25-37); 18:18-19, 39-42

Throughout the Gospel, Jesus repeatedly answers a question with a question. He seems to be doing so for two reasons:

• To point out the false assumptions in the question he's been asked.

• To move the conversation on to his agenda, rather than the questioner's.

Answering a question with a question challenges people. It reminds us that what matters is not how Jesus answers our questions, but how we answer his. Think about how you talk about your faith with others.

❷ *How could you follow Jesus' example and use helpful questions to respond to their questions?*

··

❷ *What is Jesus' question (v 4)?*

❷ *How does this thwart his opponents (v 5-6)?*

Fear of the truth had prevented them recognising that John was sent by God. Fear of man now stops them saying that he wasn't a prophet. Their final response in verse 7 is almost comic in its uselessness! But Jesus' question is even cleverer than that. He is lining himself up with John, saying: *The answer to where my authority comes from is the same as the answer to where John's authority came from.* If they're not going to confront and wrestle with the truth about John, they won't be able to grasp the truth about Jesus (v 8).

☑ Apply

❷ *Why is it wonderfully liberating to have accepted who Jesus is, rather than trying to resist it?*
❷ *Are there ways in which:*
   • *you are resisting the truth about who Jesus is or what he teaches?*
   • *you act more out of fear of men than out of a desire to please him?*

⬈ Pray

Thank God that he has told us who Jesus is and where his authority to teach is from. Pray that you would listen to, and live with, Jesus as your King. Ask for his help in doing so when it goes against the expectations or demands of those around you.

Tenancy disagreement

The religious leaders have fired their first shot (v 2), and missed. Now Jesus responds, via a parable. It's his commentary on what is going to happen in the next few days.

Vineyard

Read Luke 20:9-16

God often pictures his people and his land as a vineyard (see, for instance, Isaiah 5:1-2). So does Jesus (Luke 13:6-9). Here, the vineyard is the land; the "farmers" (20:9) are the leaders, and the people, of Israel; and the vineyard owner is, of course, God himself.

> ❷ *Why is the landlord's action in verse 10 fair?*
> ❷ *How do the tenants' responses spiral downwards (v 10-12)?*

The expected answer to the owner's question in v 13 is: "Kick the tenants out!"

> ❷ *What does he do instead? How is this undeserved kindness?*

The tenants' response (v 14-15) is both considered and deliberate. With tragic logic, they kill the heir to keep the land. They will be masters of this vineyard...

> ❷ *...or will they (v 15-16)?*
> ❷ *What is Jesus saying will be happening spiritually as he is arrested, tried and executed in Jerusalem, the capital of God's land?*

Again, we see the grace of God in verse 16. He will still have people in his vineyard. There will still be tenants to enjoy life in his place of abundance. But they will be "others" (v 16).

Building

Read Luke 20:17-19

It must be an unnerving experience to have the Lord of creation look directly at you (v 17)! Jesus, the "son" of the first parable, now pictures himself as a building brick as he quotes from the Psalms.

> ❷ *What point is he making in verse 17?*
> ❷ *What warning is he issuing in verse 18?*

There's great irony in verse 19. The leaders know the parable is aimed primarily at them—Jesus has hit the target. But in their determination to shut Jesus up, they continue to act the part Jesus has laid out for them. Tragically, they will kill the heir to shut him out of his world—and they will face the judgment of verse 16.

▾ Apply

> ❷ *How is this parable a warning to us as those who consider ourselves God's people today?*
> ❷ *How is it a reminder of God's grace?*

···· **TIME OUT** ·······························

Read 1 Peter 2:4-8

> ❷ *How do God's true people relate to the Son, to Jesus the capstone/cornerstone (v 4-5)?*
> ❷ *How will you live sacrificially today?*

The image issue

Jerusalem was a whirlwind of political conflict. The Romans were in military charge; the Jewish leaders were in religious control.

....

The Jews hated the Romans, but had no choice but to submit to their rule. What the people most wanted was a liberator to free them from the Roman leader Caesar.

A brilliant question

To oppose Roman rule was to invite arrest and an execution. To support it was to incite a riot and a lynching.

Read Luke 20:20-22

- ❓ *Why is the spies' question in verse 22 extremely clever?*
- ❓ *How is Jesus praised in verse 21?*
- ❓ *Who is saying this (v 20-21)? Are they being sincere?*
- ❓ *Saying nice things to or about Jesus while opposing his rule over us— how do we see this attitude today?*
- ❓ *Do you ever find yourself doing it? How, and why?*

An even-better answer

Read Luke 20:23-26

- ❓ *How does Jesus avoid both inflaming the Roman authorities and the Jewish crowd?*

There's a clear application here: unless they are asking us to disobey God, it is right to live under the authorities that have been placed over us—even if we don't like them or agree with them! We're to pay our taxes!

But there's more here—and as so often, the key is not in the question others ask Jesus, but in the question Jesus asks them.

- ❓ *What question does he ask in verse 24?*

"Inscription" is literally "image".

- ❓ *Why does the denarius belong to Caesar (v 24-25)?*

And so it should be given back to Caesar in the way that he asks—taxation.

Read Genesis 1:26-27

- ❓ *What bears God's image?*
- ❓ *So who do we belong to?*

And so all that we have and are should be given to God. When Jesus says in Luke 20:25: "Give ... to God what is God's", he means *you. All* of you.

🔼 Pray

Lord, thank you that you made me in your image. Thank you for the dignity and value this gives me. Help me to draw my sense of who I am from the truth about whose I am. Amen.

🔽 Apply

- ❓ *Is there any part of your life you're holding back from God?*
- ❓ *How would your life be different this week if you gave to God what belongs to him in that area of life?*

Bible in a year: Job 32-33 • 1 Corinthians 11:1-16

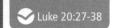
Better than we understand

The next salvo against Jesus sounds very modern in its sneery, superior tone…

Read Luke 20:27

❷ *What did the Sadducees believe?*

These men were the religious elite, who ran temple worship. They saw only the first five books of the Old Testament as God's word, and rejected virtually any idea of the supernatural or life beyond death.

Ridiculous?

Read Luke 20:28-33

In Israel, in order to carry on the family line, a childless widow would marry her dead husband's brother (v 28).

❷ *How does the Sadducees' imaginary scenario make the idea of resurrection seem foolish?*

This woman was either very unfortunate, or she liked to cook with arsenic! But the point is serious: come on, Jesus, the notion of resurrection is ridiculous!

Real!

Read Luke 20:34-38

❷ *What is Jesus' answer (v 34-36)?*
❷ *What is exciting about Jesus' description of life beyond death for a believer (v 36)?*

Resurrection life isn't ridiculous, even if we don't know exactly what it will be like. What is ridiculous is refusing to accept something is true simply because we can't see it, or understand it. Reality is not limited to what our reasoning can fathom!

❷ *How does this reassure you in the face of aggressive atheists' attacks on our faith?*

⌃ Pray

Thank God for resurrection life. Thank him that it will be better than even the best this life has given you, better than you can even imagine. Ask for its prospect to excite and encourage you today.

···· **TIME OUT** ··

"No marriage in heaven" can be a troubling idea for a happily married Christian to hear and be glad about. **Read Revelation 19:6-9.**

The marriage of Jesus the Lamb to Christians—"the saints" (ESV)—is the ultimate marriage, bringing a joy which the happiness of the best human marriage is merely a glimpse of. That's because this spouse is not only wonderful, he's perfect. Jesus gives us what no other person can. He loves us better than anyone else ever will. He deserves our greatest love. So it's being with him that should most thrill us when we think of heaven. And, if our spouse is a believer, we can be thrilled that one day they'll be married to Jesus, not to us!

This may not be easy. But we can trust that the God of the living knows what he is doing. *Why not speak to him now?*

Someone to shout about

Raised voices can mean many things: a shouted warning of danger, anger or even cheering for a sports team. But maybe there's another reason to shout…

Shout!

Read Psalm 66:1-4

- ❓ *What are the reasons why our God is so worthy of praise (v 2-3)?*
- ❓ *To whom is the writer issuing the command of verse 1?*

⌄ Apply

If that's a command to everyone, including you and me, then I guess *Explore* should encourage you to be obedient. You may be having a quiet time, but perhaps it should turn into a noisy time! Go on—shout for joy to God!

- ❓ *Did you feel a bit embarrassed? Why?*

Are there bad, as well as good, reasons why most of us would blush at the thought of shouting out loud? We shout for our football or rugby teams; perhaps we feel that such outward enthusiasm is out of place with our great and holy God. Read Matthew 21:14-16 and reassess that attitude…

Sea why

Read Psalm 66:5-15

Verse 1 calls on the whole earth to praise God because what he has done has world-wide significance.

- ❓ *But what is verse 6 referring to (see Exodus 14)?*

- ❓ *And why should everyone praise God, according to Psalm 66:7?*
- ❓ *But what else does the writer know comes from God (v 11, 12a)?*
- ❓ *And where, wonderfully, does it lead (v 10, 12b)?*

⌃ Pray

As then, so now. The way to the promised land is through the desert of testing, and the trial of suffering. It was the way for the Lord Jesus also. Give praise that he went through it for us.

Sure faith…

Read Psalm 66:16-20

The writer wants to give his "testimony" to the people: to tell them what God has done for him, so that they too will be encouraged. Not only is the Lord the God of the nations, who held back the sea to save his people, but he answers the prayers of one individual.

- ❓ *What was it that allowed God to hear David's prayer (v 18, 19)?*

Jesus *saw*

Two surprising things happen now. Some religious leaders actually agree with Jesus. Then, he finds something on the Temple Mount that pleases him.

Not just a teacher

Read Luke 20:39-44

Think back to yesterday's wrestle over the resurrection.

> ❓ *How do the teachers of the law respond to Christ's victory over the Sadducees (v 39)?*

Could it be that the religious opposition to the Lord Jesus is beginning to soften?

> ❓ *What question does he respond with (v 41)?*

In Jewish society, sons deferred to fathers. No son could be his father's "Lord". If the Christ, God's promised King, is "only" the son of David... then, asks Jesus, why does David call him "Lord" (v 44)? Jesus is saying, *You admit I am a good teacher (v 39). But your category for me is far too small. Even if you conceded I am the son of David, you'd still be failing to see who I am. David himself called me Lord, just as he called God Lord (v 42). So,* Jesus says, *If you don't know me as your God, you don't know me at all.*

Not like the teachers

Read Luke 20:45 – 21:4

> ❓ *What does Jesus criticise the teachers of the law for (v 46-47)?*
> ❓ *What is their religious activity aimed at achieving?*
> ❓ *What is the widow praised for (21:2-4)?*

Jesus deliberately draws a contrast between the impressive teachers of the law and the unnoticed poor widow.

> ❓ *What is he telling us about true commitment to God?*

This is all addressed to the disciples— those who would lead the church.

> ❓ *Why do they particularly need to remember this lesson?*

⌄ Apply

It's easy to fall into the trap of doing "good" or "religious" acts because we hope other people will notice us and be impressed. One way to discern if this is our real motivation for doing something is to ask: "Would I do this if I knew no other human would ever know about it?"

> ❓ *Is this something you need to watch out for? When?*
> ❓ *How does Jesus noticing the widow's actions encourage you in your Christian life?*
> ❓ *How do the widow's actions themselves challenge you about your Christian life?*

Stand firm to the end

Earthquakes often have "foreshocks"—smaller earthquakes that can be serious in themselves. But they are signs that something even more deadly is about to come.

The idea of a serious foreshock and catastrophic mainshock is the key to understanding Luke 21.

One warning, two questions
Read Luke 21:5-7

❓ *What impresses the disciples (v 5)?*

The "Second Temple", built by King Herod to be the centre of Jewish religious and national life, was one of the most spectacular buildings in the first-century world. Begun in 20 BC, and still two decades from completion, the "stones" (v 5) were 60 feet in length. The historian Josephus described the temple as "a snow-clad mountain".

❓ *Why would Jesus' words in verse 6 have been devastating to these Christ-following Jews?*

So they ask (v 7): When will this come? And how will we know it's coming? As he answers, Jesus first points beyond the foreshock of the temple's destruction.

Mainshock: approaching the end
Read Luke 21:8-11

"The end" (v 9) is the day Christ returns.

❓ *What will happen before "the end" (v 9-11)?*

❓ *What must Christ's people be careful not to do before "the end" (v 8)?*

The Lord Jesus then, in verse 12, switches his focus back to the foreshock.

Foreshock: the temple's end
Read Luke 21:12-19

❓ *What will happen to Jesus' people before the destruction of the temple (v 12-17)?*
❓ *How is verse 19 both a challenge and a huge encouragement to the disciples?*

Verse 19 makes sense of verse 18. These first Christians will be tried, tortured, even executed. But their eternal health is secure—as long as they stand firm in their allegiance to their Lord and Saviour.

☑ Apply

Jesus is setting two events side by side— the serious foreshock of the temple's destruction, and the catastrophic mainshock at "the end". The foreshock shows us what the mainshock will be like.

Around the world, verses 12-19 are happening today. Perhaps you experience something of them at work, at home, with friends.

❓ *What will it look like for you to stay "standing firm" today?*

Stand up to look forward

Jesus has outlined what will happen before the destruction of the Jerusalem Temple, and before the end of this world. Today, he explains what those actual events will be like.

Foreshock: desolation

Read Luke 21:20-24

> ❓ *What is going to happen to Israel's capital? Why (v 22)?*
> ❓ *The serious foreshock is a small taste of the mainshock. What are we learning about what "the end" will bring?*

This foreshock happened in AD 70, when Roman armies surrounded, besieged, invaded and sacked Jerusalem. In fact, Jesus is giving the child-friendly account of events. The full details of massacres, rapes and cannibalism are truly horrendous. And verse 22 makes clear *this is all divine punishment.* So we need to bear in mind that it didn't have to be like this...

Read Luke 19:41-44

Jerusalem could have enjoyed peace (v 42), most importantly with God but also with the world. But it rejected the offer.

> ❓ *How did it do this (end of v 44)?*

When we consider the horror of AD 70, we must remember that God's Son came to this city. And they threw him out; nailed him to a cross; killed him, so they did not have to have him in their midst.

> ❓ *What does this tell us about God's judgment?*

Mainshock: shaken

Read Luke 21:25-31

Here, Jesus seems to have moved on from the foreshock to the mainshock.

> ❓ *What will happen to creation (v 25-26)?*
> ❓ *How will people react (v 26)?*
> ❓ *And if they thought that was terrifying, what will they also see (v 27)?*

If you have spent your years shutting Jesus out of your life and out of his world, this is the most terrifying sight possible. But not all people need to fear...

> ❓ *What should Jesus' followers who are alive at this point do (v 28)?*

⌄ Apply

In every generation, including ours, we see glimmers of verses 25-26. Nations in conflict. Nature out of control. Feeling apprehensive about our world. These do not mean the end has come, or will come in our lifetime; but they do remind us that it will come.

> ❓ *When you see those glimmers, how should you respond (v 28)?*

For the Christian, there is no need to fear the future. The return of the Son of Man does not mean horrendous judgment for his people. It brings redemption— glorious freedom.

> ❓ *What could you work on worrying about less? How will you "stand up" and look towards redemption today?*

Stand before the Son

Jerusalem in AD 70 stands as a historical monument to the reality of God's judgment. Now the Son of God focuses on God's future judgment.

It will happen
Read Luke 21:32-33

"This generation" (v 32) could mean those who see the signs of verses 25-26 will still be alive when the Son of Man comes (v 27). But it probably means that this age—between his first coming and his return—won't end till these things happen.

❓ *How does verse 33…*
- *give us confidence that we can trust Jesus' words in Luke 21?*
- *show us what will change in that final judgment, and what won't?*

···· **TIME OUT** ································

Read Revelation 21:1-7

There is a future beyond "the end". Destruction is part of God's renewal of his creation.

❓ *Which sentence in this passage particularly excites you today?*

It can trap you
Read Luke 21:34-38

When the foreshock hit, some left their houses, and all they owned, to stand outside, ready for the mainshock. When it came, they weren't trapped.

❓ *How might we be trapped (v 34-35)?*

The temptation will always be to focus our attention on the present, wrenching our

gaze from the future. They stop us being ready every day for the Son of Man's coming (17:30-32). They trap us.

❓ *What should we do instead (21:36)?*
❓ *What will we then be able to do (v 36b)?*

Stand
Read Luke 21:19, 28, 36

Luke 21 can seem confusing, or worrying, or both! But the instruction of Christ to his people is actually remarkably simple. Final, catastrophic judgment is coming: so stay standing. Stand firm in your faith when persecution comes. Stand up and look towards the end when this world goes wrong. Look forward to standing before the Son of Man as your friend, not your foe, when he returns. Whatever happens around us and to us, all we need do is stand!

⌃ Pray

Thank Jesus that he is in control of the future. Thank him that he has secured your future for you. Thank him that you can look forward to perfection, not judgment.

Ask him to keep you standing firm in faith now, so you can stand before him in joy then.

Betrayed

As we reach the last 48 hours of the Lord Jesus' life, the pace of the narrative slows, and the tension rises…

Jesus in Jerusalem

As Luke begins his account of the "passion", we're at stalemate. Jesus has entered Jerusalem as the King (Luke 19:28-38)—but Jerusalem doesn't want him (19:39-44). The religious leaders are set on killing Jesus (19:47; 20:19), but they're concerned about the reaction of the crowd if they arrest him in public (19:48, 20:19). They won't be moved in their opposition to Jesus of Nazareth— but they don't dare make a move on him.

Something has to give. And something does.

Then Satan…

Read Luke 22:1-6

Satan hasn't appeared since 4:1-13, when his attempts to convince Jesus to be a king under his influence, rather than under God's rule, failed. Thwarted, "he left him until an opportune time" (v 13). And this is that time.

- ❷ *What does Satan do (22:3)?*
- ❷ *What is shocking about…*
  - *who Judas is (v 3)?*
  - *what he does (v 4)?*
  - *what he does it for (v 5)?*
- ❷ *How does Judas' offer break the stalemate (v 6)?*
- ❷ *Who now appears to have the upper hand in the battle between Jesus and his human foes, and the struggle between the Son of God and his cosmic enemy?*

Judas was directed by Satan; but he was not dictated to by him. He could have resisted, just as Jesus had. But he chose not to.

It's a chilling moment. Here is Judas, a man who followed Jesus, who professed loyalty to Jesus, who knew and ate with and laughed with Jesus, who witnessed his power and love firsthand. And then who betrayed him.

⌄ Apply

Perhaps Luke is challenging us to ask ourselves: Could I be like Judas? How might being the centre of attention, being feted by human power or being lured by wealth cause me to forsake my Lord?

- ❷ *What is your considered answer to those questions?*

⌃ Pray

"For a good person someone might possibly dare to die. But … while we were still sinners, Christ died for us" (Romans 5:7-8).

Thank Jesus that there is no sin his blood cannot cover, no betrayal his death cannot blot out. Ask him to forgive how you have betrayed him in the past; and ask him to change you so that you will not do so today.

Knowing where to look

Then came the day on which the Passover lamb had to be sacrificed. But very soon, a Passover lamb unlike any other would be sacrificed…

The meal

Read Exodus 12:21-30

- ❓ *What was the Passover meal a reminder of (v 26-27)? What was to be talked about during the meal?*
- ❓ *What did the death of a lamb achieve at the first Passover, when God's people were still slaves in Egypt (v 21-23)?*

Read Luke 22:7-13

- ❓ *Why do you think Luke mentions "Passover" four times here?*

Looking forward

Read Luke 22:14-19

- ❓ *Why did Jesus "eagerly desire" to share this particular Passover with his friends (v 16, 18)?*
- ❓ *What must happen between this Passover meal and the next one that Jesus will share with his friends (end v 15)?*

Looking back

Read Luke 22:20-23

The core ingredients of a Passover meal were bread, wine and the lamb. Each helped God's people look back to the night God rescued them from his judgment, bringing them into relationship—covenant—with him. But as Jesus explains this Passover meal, he doesn't look towards the lamb's blood on the doorframes in Egypt…

- ❓ *What does he say the bread is a picture of (v 19)? And the wine (v 20)?*

Luke doesn't mention the lamb. Because the lamb at this Passover meal is not *on* the table, but *at* the table. The eternal, all-powerful, Son of Man (Daniel 7:13-14) is also the Lamb who will suffer, be torn apart, be poured out for his people.

☑ Apply

Two thousand years later, we still share this meal, obeying Jesus' command to "do this in remembrance of me".

- ❓ *What should we think about as we share Communion?*
- ❓ *How might we feel as we think about those things?*

Judas is still present at this meal (Luke 22:21- 22). But what lies ahead for him is not eating with Jesus in his kingdom but "woe". What matters is not eating the meal with our mouths, but believing in what it points us to in our hearts.

◣ Pray

Christians will eat this meal for eternity. For now, as we share it our death lies ahead of us. One day, we will share it with our death behind us! Thank Jesus that, because he is the Lamb who died for us, our death will not be the end of our sharing his Supper.

A world of difference

A psalm with just seven verses? And two of them are the same? It would be easy to read it quickly, and not savour the significance...

Question time

Read Psalm 67

This psalm is a prayer. To work out what it's about, answer these seven questions:

- ❓ *Who's doing the praying?*
- ❓ *What for?*
- ❓ *Is there a verse which seems to sum it up?*
- ❓ *What's the psalm telling us about God?*
- ❓ *What's it saying about his people?*
- ❓ *What's it saying about his world?*
- ❓ *Which verse particularly hits you? Why?*

Verse 1 quotes the first words of a prayer that was said for God's Old Testament people (see Numbers 6:22-27). It's picture language, but beautiful.

- ❓ *Think what it would mean for God's people to have God's face "shine" upon them.*
- ❓ *If that happened, what would follow?*
- ❓ *Do you see the link with Psalm 67:2?*

God's people would "reflect" God to the world and make his rescue known to everybody. Verse 2 sums it up best.

- ❓ *Then what would happen (v 3-5, 6-7)?*

⌄ Apply

God chose a people for himself (the Israelites) in order to make himself known to the nations. The very purpose of blessing his people was so that the rest of the world might know the glory of God, and come to honour him.

- ❓ *So, if you have been blessed by God in any way—talents, money, position, friends, family—what does he want to achieve with those blessings?*

Through his people, God reaches those who don't know him. That's been his way all along.

⌃ Pray

Pray through verses 1 and 2. It's not wrong to ask for God's blessing. It is wrong to think that the blessing he gives us is for us to enjoy alone.

Pray that verse 7 would become a reality through your witness, and the witness of your church.

The Lord who serves

We live in an age of league tables. Do you ever wonder where you rank when it comes to discipleship? Ever rate yourself highly (and smugly) or low down (and sadly)?

Not like that
Read Luke 22:24-26

> ❓ *Given what Jesus has just been talking about, why is the argument in verse 24 horribly inappropriate?*

I wonder if there was a note of weariness in Jesus' answer. He is preparing to die for these men—and all they do is squabble over the discipleship pecking order.

> ❓ *Whose mindset does he say they are following (v 25)?*

What insight Jesus has in verse 25! In our world, we love to grab prestige and status to enjoy for ourselves, while portraying it as service of others. It's not only politicians who do this. It's in my heart as I preach in church, or get my name on the front of a book. It's present in flower guilds, and scout troops, and school hierarchies. The power may be less than a "king": the attitude is the same.

> ❓ *But—how does Jesus measure greatness (v 26)?*

The greatest Christian service is quiet, humble and often unnoticed

⌄ Apply

> ❓ *Do you ever struggle with a verse-25 attitude? When, and how?*
> ❓ *As you humbly serve your church, how does verse 26 encourage you?*

Who is greater?
Read Luke 22:27-30

> ❓ *What has Jesus come to his world to do (v 27)?*

Imagine a G20 summit of world leaders. The limos arrive. The politicians enter the banqueting hall. But the US President is nowhere to be seen. Then the British Prime Minister goes into the bathroom—and there's the President, cleaning the toilets. That's an inadequate picture of what the eternal Son of God did in his earthly life.

> ❓ *Jesus did not come to get, but to give. And what does he give his followers (v 29-30)?*

We should serve and wait on him (17:7-10). That would be an eternal privilege—to be allowed to serve the King of the cosmos! But our Lord gives us so much more. In eternity, he will say to his people, *Come and sit. Come and dine with me. Come and share in my rule over my world.*

⌄ Apply

> ❓ *How do these verses change your view of serving others?*
> ❓ *How will the Lord's example (v 27), and his gift (v 29), change your attitude to the Christian life this week?*

Our defeat, his victory

A cosmic battle is raging. Like it or not, we're on the front line. Satan has pulled Judas away from loving Jesus. His next attack is coming…

The enemy
Read Luke 22:31

> ❓ *What does Jesus know?*

"Sift you as wheat" was a saying which meant "take you apart". Simon Peter will be the next target. But the "you" here is plural. Satan attacks any and every believer, any chance he gets.

Our General
Read Luke 22:32, 35-38

> ❓ *What does Jesus say he has done (v 32)?*
> ❓ *What does he tell Simon to do beyond the attack (v 32)?*

Jesus knows Peter will be defeated. He will fail the coming test—he will need to turn back to Jesus. But wonderfully, he will turn back, because Jesus has asked his Father to make sure Peter's faith will not fail.

> ❓ *What is about to happen to Jesus (v 37)?*

Read Isaiah 53:12

Jesus is talking about what will happen as he pours out his life unto death.

> ❓ *What will he bear in his death?*

Intercession means to speak up for someone successfully; transgressors means people who have failed to live God's way.

> ❓ *What will his death enable Jesus to do?*

When Peter, and when we, fail to resist the devil, we can look to the one who defeated sin and death, Satan's two great weapons; to the one who is able to say to his Father, *This one's mine. I've taken her judgment, I've died her death. Satan has no claim on her.* When we fail, we look in faith to the one who did not fail.

My own General?
Read Luke 22:33-38

> ❓ *How confident is Peter (v 33)?*

Like Peter, we love to think we can be good Christian soldiers. We will fight and win for Jesus! But Peter will learn the humbling lesson that the Christian life is about how Jesus has fought, and won, for failures.

🔼 Pray

Thank Jesus for dying for your failures; he is able to pray effectively that your faith in him will not fail.

Ask Jesus to show you where you are under attack, and to give you the strength you don't naturally have, to stand against the enemy.

🔽 Apply

> ❓ *Are you humbly honest with other Christians about times you've failed and then turned back, so that you can strengthen them to do the same when they fail (v 32)?*

Bible in a year: Proverbs 13-15 • Titus 2

Jesus in anguish

It's not often that the Gospel writers tell us how Jesus felt. When they do, it should make us sit up and take notice. And it should change how we feel too.

The prayer

Read Luke 22:39-46

> ❓ *How is Jesus feeling?*
> ❓ *Why does he seem to be feeling like this?*

Read Isaiah 51:17; Ezekiel 23:28-34

> ❓ *What does this "cup" contain? What happens to those who drink from it?*

And this is the cup Jesus knew he would drink from as he died the next day.

> ❓ *Why is the beginning of his prayer (Luke 22:42) completely understandable?*
> ❓ *How is the end of his prayer (v 42) absolutely amazing?*

To give us the cup of the new covenant (v 20), to make it possible for us to drink with him in his eternal kingdom (v 30), Christ must first drink our cup. The cup he does not deserve, should not drink and recoils physically from. It's the cup which he will nevertheless drink from, so that we don't have to. As he begins to confront its horror, the shedding of his blood begins (v 44). The Father wills it. The Son is committed to it. For the first, last and only time in eternity, the Son will not experience the Father's love. Instead, he'll know his Father's wrath.

⌃ Pray

Re-read v 41-44 and say to yourself, *He did this for me. He felt this for me. He took the cup meant for me.* Thank him with all your heart.

The sleep

> ❓ *What temptations are Christ's disciples going to face soon, do you think?*
> ❓ *What does Jesus know they need (v 40)?*
> ❓ *What do they do instead (v 45)?*

At the moment their Master most needs their support, at the time they most need God's help themselves—they go to sleep! And despite their exhaustion, Jesus doesn't leave them to regain physical energy—he warns them that they most need spiritual strengthening (v 46).

⌄ Apply

> ❓ *When you know tomorrow will be difficult or busy, which do you most make sure you try to get:*
>   • *a good night's sleep?*
>   • *a proper time of prayer?*
> ❓ *How will Jesus' prayer in verse 42 shape what you ask God for next time you face a time of trial?*

⌄ Apply

Lord, naturally I want to have an easy, comfortable, healthy, successful day today. But I would rather that your will be done than my desires are met. If your plan requires me to go through difficulty, discomfort, pain and disappointment, your will be done. Amen.

When darkness reigns

As you read the verses, pick out where you can see hypocrisy, cowardice and love.

The friends

Read Luke 22:47-53

Jesus has pointed his friends to Isaiah 53:12 (Luke 22:37); he has prayed, presumably aloud, of his willingness to drink the cup of God's wrath (v 42). He knows, and has explained, that he must die (e.g. 18:31-33).

> ❷ *But what do his followers do (22:49-50)?*
> ❷ *What is their aim, do you think?*

It's an understandable reaction. But it's the wrong one. It seems brave, but it isn't. True courage under pressure is not fighting our way out—it's following God's will, wherever it leads.

This is still a challenge for we who call ourselves Jesus' followers today. If I had been there that day, I think I would have run away. Perhaps I would have fought back. But would I have been like Jesus, accepting God's will, walking into the fire of suffering and death, trusting that my Father knows what he is doing?

⌄ Apply

> ❷ *When do you find it easy to take matters into your own hands, rather than obeying God's will and word?*
> ❷ *Next time you are under pressure, how will you remember to do what God asks, however hard?*

The Lord

Re-read Luke 22:47-53

> ❷ *How does Jesus respond to his followers' actions (v 51)?*

Remember, Jesus is in spiritual agony (v 44). He's just been betrayed by a close friend (v 47-48). And the high priest's servant is there to arrest him so that he can be whipped, stripped and killed.

> ❷ *How does verse 51 show the astonishing love of Jesus?*
> ❷ *How is it a lesson to his disciples?*

It is the hour "when darkness reigns" (v 53). The disciples had tried to fight the darkness. Jesus simply got on with loving people in the darkness.

And as he heals this enemy's ear, the Lord practises what he had preached (6:32-36); and he provides a picture of what he will do the next day, when he will die in the place of those who have made themselves his enemies.

⌃ Pray

Thank Jesus for his love for his enemies. Thank him that in the darkness of the cross, he hung there for you and me, loving us until his last breath so that we might have healing and life.

 Bible in a year: Proverbs 19-20 • Hebrews 1

Feeling the failure

There are few episodes in Scripture more tragic than this one. Jesus is under arrest and about to be on trial for his life. Within hours, he will be dead.

But he should be able to rely on one friend to stand by him: Peter, who has declared: "I am ready to go with you to prison and to death" (22:33).

The failure

Read Luke 22:54-60

Round the table with fellow followers of Jesus, Peter had been confident.

- ❓ *What happens round the fireplace with potential foes of Jesus?*
- ❓ *Why is it significant that Peter reacts the same way more than once?*

Peter had an hour between his first two failures, and his third (v 59). He had time to think, to regret, to change. He didn't.

- ❓ *Why is the end of verse 60 significant (look back to:34)?*
- ❓ *What does it tell us about Jesus?*

⌄ Apply

It is much easier to pledge loyalty to Jesus with his people on a Sunday than with co-workers or with non-believing friends in the middle of the week.

- ❓ *When are the times you are most tempted to keep quiet about knowing Jesus, or deny it outright?*
- ❓ *How could you stand up for your Lord in those moments?*

Read Luke 22:61-62

"The Lord turned and looked straight at Peter." Surely this is the most awful moment of Peter's life. He has consciously, decisively and utterly failed his Lord and friend— and on the night he needed him most.

- ❓ *Why is his response totally correct?*

I am far too quick to excuse or downplay my failures to live and speak for Jesus; far too quick to move on from them. Peter challenges me to ask not: "Have I failed Jesus?" (I have), but: "Have I felt the weight of that—have I wept about that?"

⌃ Pray

- ❓ *Are there things you need to weep over?*

Having done so, thank Jesus that he did what we cannot do—that while Peter denied him, he continued to walk to the cross, where he would die for all Peter's failures, and all of ours too.

The future

Four days after Peter failed his Lord, a couple of Jesus' friends met the other disciples with some exciting news—they had met the once-dead, now-risen, Jesus.

Read Luke 24:33-34

- ❓ *Why do you think Luke includes the detail at the end of verse 34? What is wonderful about it?*

Praise God that he is the friend of failures!

SUPERB OUTREACH BOOK FOR EASTER

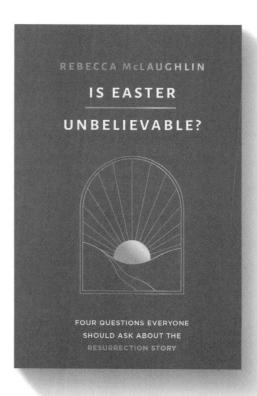

In this concise book, respected apologist Rebecca McLaughlin outlines the evidence that Jesus really did rise from the dead and why it's the best news ever.

Ideal to give away at Easter outreach services and events, as well as to give to new Christians wanting to remind themselves of the evidence for their faith.

thegoodbook.co.uk/is-easter-unbelievable
thegoodbook.com/is-easter-unbelievable

Introduce a friend to

explore

If you're enjoying using *Explore*, why not introduce a friend? *Time with God* is our introduction to daily Bible reading and is a great way to get started with a regular time with God. It includes 28 daily readings along with articles, advice and practical tips on how to apply what the passage teaches.

Why not order a copy for someone you would like to encourage?

Coming up next…

❤ Easter from Luke's Gospel
with Carl Laferton

❤ Esther
with Tim Thornborough

❤ Mark
with Jason Meyer and Katy Morgan

❤ 2 Peter and Jude
with Miguel Nuñez

 Don't miss your copy. Contact your local Christian bookshop or church agent, or visit:

UK & Europe: thegoodbook.co.uk
info@thegoodbook.co.uk
Tel: 0333 123 0880

North America: thegoodbook.com
info@thegoodbook.com
Tel: 866 244 2165

Australia & New Zealand:
thegoodbook.com.au
info@thegoodbook.com.au
Tel: (02) 9564 3555

India: thegoodbook.co.in
info@thegoodbook.co.in
Tel: (+44) 0333 123 0880

South Africa: thegoodbook.co.za
info@thegoodbook.co.za

Join the *explore* community

The *Explore* Facebook group is a community of people who use *Explore* to study the Bible each day.

This is the place to share your thoughts, questions, encouragements and prayers as you read *Explore*, and interact with other readers, as well as contributors, from around the world. No questions are too simple or too difficult to ask.

JOIN NOW:
facebook.com/groups/tgbc.explore